EAVESDROPPING
ON THE
ECHOES

EAVESDROPPING
ON THE
ECHOES

VOICES FROM THE OLD TESTAMENT

Ted Loder

RELEASED

LIBRARY OF
FIRST UNITED METHODIST CHURCH
BURLINGTON, VERMONT.

San Diego, California

LuraMedia™

Other books by Ted Loder:
Guerrillas of Grace: Prayers for the Battle
No One But Us: Personal Reflections on Public Sanctuary
Tracks in the Straw: Tales Spun from the Manger

Eavesdropping on the Echoes is also available on cassette tape.

© Copyright 1987 LuraMedia
San Diego, California
International Copyright Secured
Publisher's Catalog Number LM-606
Printed and Bound in the United States of America

LuraMedia
P.O. 261668
7060 Miramar Road, Ste. 104
San Diego, CA 92121

Library of Congress Cataloging-in-Publication Data

Loder, Ted, 1930–
    Eavesdropping on the echoes.

    1. Story sermons—Collected works. 2. Sermons, American—Collected
works. I. Title.

BV4307.S7L63	1987	220.9'505	87-21526

ISBN 0-931055-59-x

The Scripture quotations from The Revised Standard Version of the Bible,
copyright 1946, 1952, 1971 by the Division of Christian Education of the National
Council of the Churches of Christ in the U.S.A., are used by permission.

The Scripture quotations from The New English Bible, © copyright 1961, 1970 by
the Delegates of the Oxford University Press and the Syndics of the Cambridge
University Press, are reprinted by permission.

For
Theodore William and Bess Mary Pflug Loder—
        the beloved ones who went before. . .
Lyle Loder Friedman and the nameless children's children—
        the eager ones who come after. . .
                and
all the gracious echoes. . .

CONTENTS

COCKING THE EAR,
CLEARING THE THROAT:
A PREFACE

Years ago I heard a story about a seminary student who approached Paul Tillich following one of that great theologian's lectures. The student clutched a Bible which he thrust at Dr. Tillich while angrily asking, "Is this the inspired word of God or not?" Dr. Tillich smiled at the student and calmly replied, "It is if it grasps you rather than you grasping it."

Eavesdropping on the Echoes reveals something of how I have been grasped by the biblical word, particularly by twelve characters in the Old Testament. Originally written as narrative sermons for public worship, the stories have been re-written for this book. Though presented as monologues or soliloquies, they are actually dialogues, first and most obviously between the biblical word and me. Hopefully, that level of dialogue reflects why I find Tillich's reply to the student an accurate, liberating and compelling view of Scripture.

Being grasped by the biblical word is both illuminating and befuddling—and why wouldn't it be, given the character of the grasper and the grasped? It is not an easy or simple process. Karl Barth, another of those seminal theologians of a generation ago, wrote compellingly of "entering the strange world of the Bible." But critical as the movement to enter the biblical world is, it can—and for many has—become a form of escapism from the struggles and discoveries of the contemporary world, our particular historical time and place. Such escapism is not only spiritually crippling, but is also a perversion of the integrity of the biblical word which is rooted in and addressed to history and the creatures who reside therein.

So the other movement of the dialogue is to invite, yea to insist, that the biblical word enter this strange contemporary world of ours. Dialogue is to hear and be confronted by the hard truth of the biblical word, *and*, in turn, to confront that word with the hard truth of the questions, observations, struggles of our experience in a world not altogether similar to that ancient biblical world. Some people will object by arguing that such insistence results in taking liberties with the text, or in reading things into the Scriptures, or, in the case of the narratives of this book, forcing autobiographical material on biblical persons. There is some truth in those objections, but they are unavoidable. Anyone who interprets anything, including the Bible, does so from his or her own perspective and experience.

But my confidence, my faith, is that the biblical word itself also invites, yea insists, on just that kind of dialogue because it is alive and dynamic. The Bible is not a reference book so much as a book of clues in a treasure hunt. It opens new areas for exploration rather than closing life off behind a fence of infallible answers. Or as someone said, "The Bible witnesses to God's ongoing effort to take away our sins, not our minds."

Biblical scholars are now saying that each variety of material or story in the Bible is multi-dimensional or plura-significant so that a text can mean many things, make many points. In a dialogue with the biblical word, we bring our own limited truth in the effort to discover, however partially, one or two of the many truths of the text. That effort is certainly one purpose of this book.

Biblical scholars also have long since given up the search for the "historical Jesus"—and, I assume, the search for a good many other historical persons of the Bible. Instead, the scholars are asking, "What kind of person, in his impact on others, prompted the witness made to him in the New Testament?" That seems to me a profoundly accurate question. By itself, it offers another purpose of this book, though I would reformulate the question into the version which I also and more specifically struggle with on these pages: "As a result of their impact on me through the biblical word, what kind of witness can I make to these persons who walk, or in some cases tiptoe, across and out of the pages of the Old Testament?"

Additionally, if somewhat less obviously, these "soliloquies" are a dialogue between other people and me. Other people include those teachers, friends and adversaries who constitute a portion of my "great cloud of witnesses," many of whom are the congregation who heard the original presentation of these stories as the sermon during Sunday worship. In my judgment, any sermon worth the name is dialogical, even if at the time of presentation most parties to the dialogue are silent in the same sense that most parties to a play are silent, though the persons on stage are enacting some part of the drama of individuals in the audience.

In essential ways the "me" in any dialogue is not solitary but corporate. Certainly that is true in these narrative sermons. They wrestle with issues which have become my issues through my involvement with others, my dialogue with others, indeed the way others have become part of who I am. A primary example of this, in these narratives, is the presentation of feminist perspectives and insights. Until my consciousness was raised, until I was grasped by the justice claim of the women's movement, I did not view feminism as my issue. Now it is mine, not only as a justice issue, but as a relational issue at both the larger communal and the personally intimate levels, even as an identity issue—i.e., "Who am I as a man?"—and, finally, profoundly, as a spiritual issue which is liberating me from discerning God in strictly, and limiting, masculine terms and images. The reader will discover other examples in these narratives of the corporate nature of the dialogue.

To acknowledge and affirm that in *Eavesdropping on the Echoes* the "me" of the dialogue is itself an echo of the dialogue between me and other people is not only an honest and realistic acknowledgment, it is a theological one. Certainly one of the foremost ways God approaches us is through the claims, confrontations and care of other human beings. Their needs, struggles and gifts are modalities of God's presence, glimmers of grace, openings to the kingdom. In my view Scripture itself verifies that on almost every page. Humanity is an instrumentality of God; individuals are collaborators in grace.

It is important to note that, of the characters presented in these twelve stories, seven are included in the genealogy of Jesus recorded in Matthew's Gospel: Isaac, Abraham, Jacob, Rahab, Obed, David, Josiah. The others—Sarah, Aaron, Mahlon, Nathan, Gomer and Hosea—are certainly in the category of human, prophetic and spiritual mothers, fathers, uncles, aunts and cousins. But for me, the point of these selections is not to suggest that these people are simply forerunners of, or witnesses to, a qualitatively distinctive and immeasurably greater person named Jesus whom many of us believe is the Christ. The point of these selections is to emphasize the incredible rootedness of grace in human persons and affairs, the amazing continuities which run from these twelve to that One and on through countless others across the ages to and through us. I constantly refer to my beloved teacher H. Richard Niebuhr's formulation that God revealed Himself/Herself uniquely but not exclusively in Jesus of Nazareth.

So the unfathomable mystery, for me, is not only the radical disjunction between God and us human beings, but also the radical conjunction. It is that paradox which I believe faith holds in tension, and which holds faith in tension. To espouse one side of the paradox to the diminution of the other is, finally, a dangerous distortion. Yet it is a temptation to which it is easy to succumb.

One way in which that distortion happens is to cast biblical characters as moral heroes, or heroes of piety or love or courage, of such proportion that they are a different breed of human than we. A friend of mine who read these narratives prior to publication said I had put the warts back on these biblical characters. I took that as a positive observation. By "re-warting" these characters (if in truth they actually needed it), by underscoring their human qualities, I was attempting two objectives: one, to include myself and us in their struggles, failures, joys, and them in ours, so as to make us all more believable and believing; two, to suggest that if the humanity of the "earthen vessels" is presented with its sad flaws *and* its wondrous beauties, the "treasure" and its ingenious and endlessly creative "power" might glow even more awesomely.* I agree with Irenaeus' words which have graced several of the bulletin covers in the church I serve: "God's glory is in man (woman) fully alive."

Finally, these narratives constitute a dialogue between God and me. While perhaps the least obvious level of the dialogue, it is to me the most important. Of all the ways a dialogue with God might take place, for me it takes sharpest form in the intense hard work of thinking and writing such material as this. It is that dialogue with the "inspired word of God" which changes the way I see and respond to things—or at least it is through that dialogical process that changes in the way I see and respond become clearer to me.

That this dialogue goes beyond the literal written word of Scripture is testimony both to the power of that word and to the ingenuity of God. One of the many ways in which "going beyond" occurs is *not* evident in these narratives, and I want to explain why it is not. Earlier I mentioned the impact of feminism on me and on my discernment of God. Some of that impact is clear in some of these stories. But in the effort to be consistent with the patriarchal situation in which these stories are set, I avoided using female nouns and pronouns in referring to God (though I do so refer to God in other kinds of sermons). In the case of these narratives, it seemed to me that female references to God would disrupt and distract, not for theological reasons but for historical ones. However, some of the ways God is experienced by the characters in this book suggests they discerned traits in Yahweh that expand the traditional masculine images in Scripture.

Is my ongoing dialogue with God only idiosyncratic? By what authority do I press to such limits? Ah, that is the ancient, crucial question asked daily in some form. Who was it said, "Every new truth begins as heresy"? Well, I do not claim anything so important as new truth in the dialogue contained in this book. But to take the question more modestly, I can say that my authority for pursuing my dialogue with God, to whatever limit it takes me, is

---

*II Corinthians 4:7

the authority rooted in the Reformation itself: namely, that authority resides in the interplay of Scripture, reason, conscience and community, or as the Wesleyan quadrilateral puts it, in Scripture, tradition, experience and reason.

The small point I would make about the large subject of authority is simply that, for me, the faculty of imagination is an essential part of reason and of experience. Without launching an involved dissertation on imagination, suffice it to say that imagination is the way we shape our dreams and preview our actions. It is a primary agent of interpretation, and truth, ultimately, is not so much factual and self-evident as it is interpretive and evocative—a summons to commitment, exploration and embodiment. Imagination is the dancing partner of faith, the guide into the unknown, the source of creativity. So, fervently do I hope that these stories are imaginative, for in that sense they will manifest my dialogue with God.

Feminist theologians, along with liberation theologians, seem to be on the cutting edge of theological reflection these days. Though my knowledge is limited, I find it provocative and congenial that feminist theologians seem to be saying that we are spiritually rooted in ''energy'' which is defined in part as spontaneity, as creativity. Those enticing terms suggest that God is experienced not just as ''creator''—a concept which overly objectifies and makes God static and past tense—but as ''creativity'' which presents God as ongoing, dynamic activity. One exciting implication of this view is that we are apprehended by God through the experience of our own creativity, the exercise of our imagination. It is in risking our creativity that we shape and are shaped by God's truth, and know God's grace.

So, trusting that grace, and grateful to those who have encouraged me in this enterprise—particularly my patient editor, Marcia Broucek; my supportive publishers, Lura Jane and Adam Geiger; and my persistently loving partner, Jan Filing—I dare this book and invite others who read it to join the dialogue.

Ted Loder

THE BUTT OF THE JOKE

Ah, the sun this season of the year moves easy as a cat in the high grass, indolent, soft as a woman's inner thigh. You can almost feel it between your fingers. And the rain, when it comes, is never in a hurry because it's a prelude to some lengthy inevitability. The scent of the cedars drifts down from the high country these days and mixes with the heavy, sweet odor of the ripe, wild grapes, and the fire feels good in the evening when the air snaps like the burning twigs. The animals are fat and ... thoughtful, somehow. Yes, that's it; I've watched them, and they are thoughtful and strangely choosy. It's a beautiful thing.

This is a good time, a good season to be alive, a good season to hunt, to track boar up on the high ridges. Once of an evening when I was following them, I came upon some springs where the water seemed as if it must have trickled pure and light off the rising moon, I swear. The taste of it was silver and shadow and full of secrets, trembly like the singing of a single bird only ... only it was my heart that I could hear so clearly as the water went down my throat. And there were wild flowers all around those springs catching the dying light just so. It was as if there were a million stars scattered all around that glen, and there were no boundaries between heaven and earth.

Ah, yes, life is so amazing! All of it! And all of us! But our lack of understanding of that mystery is sad and can lead to tragedy.

Still, even as I speak of it, I don't know if I understand how amazing life is, or I am. Yet the feeling is strong in me. And insistent.

So here I am. My name is Isaac. I am glad for my name, and I'll try to tell you why. The sun and I have danced with many seasons now, until I am left with this knobby stick as my dancing partner. Obviously, I dance more slowly than I did once, and walk more slowly, too. My enemies have not always treated me lightly, and a long time ago I fell while hunting. The healing was never quite right, so sometimes it all comes back—the stiffness and the pain—shortening my step, and my pride. I am, after all, something like this autumn season: past the spring and the summer of the time God gives to a man, a bit withered of flank perhaps, and not quite as sharp of eye or tooth as once I was. Yet, strangely, I notice more now, moving slower, my fingers extended by this wooden companion I poke with. And I'm still able to draw the bow and send the arrow straight, even if not as quickly as once I could. So I'm alive, and glad to be, and amazing, for all of that.

I'm twice amazed that I'm here at all, really. My father, Abraham, was older than I am now when I was conceived. And my mother, too! I think of that often these days as I feel the chill and watch my sons grow tall: Esau hunts with me in the day, Jacob tells me stories when we pull the tent flaps tight against the night wind. So different are my sons: one obvious as a hunting dog, the other crafty as the fox. Yet, both are my sons, both embodying a part of me, both a mixture of Rebecca and me, and still so different. I love them both, you understand. But there is a distance between us, a good distance, I think.

I know I am not the same with them. Why? Is that what makes them different, or are their differences the reason I am not the same with them? Ah, but never mind. I delight in them. And I weary of them. I do wonder how it will be for them. The older I get, the more I understand my father, though I often resist the understanding because of what it says about me.

In any case, I watch my sons and I wonder! Old questions come back to me, as a father, that once I asked as a son: Must sons live out their fathers' lives? Can fathers forgive the sons they coerce to fit their dreams? Can sons forgive the fathers to whom they mockingly submit? Fathers teach you to whittle the hunting spear, and into the scent of the shavings they mix the scent of the prey they want you to hunt. With the whisper of the knife on the wood, they whisper the stories they want you to carve with your life if you are to please them.

Is that the way of it, children spent on parents' dreams? Are we doomed to act out the drama of our parents' needs and obsessions? Are they, in turn, doomed to act out a drama of *their* parents' needs, thus forever back to God's own needs, that obsession around which the stars run their very course? Are we murdered at some moment before our time begins—at birth, at conception—when some decision is made, unknown perhaps even by the maker, because our parents are only doing what was done to them? But a decision is made, nonetheless, which says, "This is who my child will be; this is how it will be, *must be*, for this child of mine! And because it will be that way for my child, so shall it be for me as well, because the maker is made by the act of making?"

I wonder, is there a way to break out of that deathly grip? Or is that just the way it is, ordained by the God who has conceived us all? Do we perform, finally, for God's pleasure? Are we some joke who makes God laugh? I have a glimpse of an answer, elusive as the sunlight through a red leaf or a deer that melts away before you can set the arrow to the bow. Well, more than an answer, or less ... it's a story.

My father was Abraham. A long time ago he left the city of Ur, and then of Haran, and wandered around with my mother, Sarah, and some servants, and Uncle Lot and his family. Finally, Abraham settled here and founded this country. He is revered as the founder of our nation, as an heroic figure. And he truly was an amazing man. More amazing than anyone knows, than I knew, though heroes and saints look different up close: not so heroic or spotless, except maybe to themselves.

I called my father "Billy Goat," mostly behind his back, I'll admit. I used that name half in affection, half in ridicule. He sensed my ambivalence and was confused by it, especially on those rare occasions when, out of defiance—or longing—I dared to call him "Billy Goat" to his face. Of course, he didn't like the name much, but I did. I loved him and I feared him. And sometimes I hated him. I didn't understand those conflicting feelings as well then as I do now. I laughed at him much of the time; I couldn't help myself. I wanted so for him to laugh with me, and for *him* to laugh, too, but he didn't. Not until . . . but I'm getting ahead of myself.

I called him "Billy Goat" because he looked funny, like a goat: whiskers on his chin and a long nose. And I called him "Billy Goat" because he was stubborn and did stupid things all the time. For instance, during all those years he and my mother were wandering around, when they'd come to the country of some powerful king, my father would tell everyone that my mother was really his sister. He thought if he said Sarah was his wife, the king would kill him in order to have her, because my mother was such a beautiful woman. But every time he told that lie (actually, it was only a half lie, because my mother *was* his half sister), the king would take Sarah anyway, thinking she wasn't married. That caused a mess, I can tell you. But did my father learn from it? Oh no! The Old Billy Goat was always getting caught in his own traps. When I was a boy, my mother would sometimes tease him about that. We'd laugh, but he'd stalk off stiff-legged, "bahing" like an old billy goat.

I could tell story after story about my not-so-heroic father. One time he and Uncle Lot decided they would divide up the land. My stupid father gave Lot the first choice. Naturally, Lot chose the rich land of the Jordan, and we got stuck with rocky, barren Canaan. My mother would chide Abraham about that sometimes. But the Old Billy Goat would snort and carry on about his virtue in giving Lot the first choice, saying how he really got the best of the deal by having Canaan anyway. My father always saw himself as a righteous man, not a foolish one. He was hard-headed as a goat.

When I got a little older and understood about such matters, I used to tease him about being such a billy goat with women, too. He was so eager to have a child, so righteously determined to get his beloved "promised nation" started, that he forced my mother to give him her maid, Hagar, for bedding, since my mother apparently was having trouble conceiving. Then when Hagar finally conceived and had Ishmael, it turned out that my father had gotten

4

himself caught between two women. Finally, he had to send Hagar and Ishmael away to keep peace in the family.

I'd laugh at him about that, about being so lusty and getting caught in all of it, but he'd just glower and roar at me to be quiet. And when I just couldn't keep from laughing at him, he'd grab his stick and start chasing me around the camp. I think he'd have tried to bash my brains out if he could have caught me. He'd swing his stick, and I'd laugh some more because I couldn't help it. Then I'd yell, more playfully than not, ''Billy Goat, Billy Goat.'' He'd get all red in the face and wheeze and run after me, swinging until he collapsed. I'd still be laughing as I went over and picked him up and helped him home. I loved him. I wanted him to laugh with me, but . . . well, he was a hundred years old when I was born and set in his ways. Maybe he always was set in his ways. Maybe most of us are. We're such fools!

Anyway, he used to talk about how long he and my mother had waited for me, dreamed of my coming. He would sit around the fire night after night and tell me about the promise God had made to him: that his descendants someday would be more numerous than the stars in heaven or the sand on the sea shore; that he would be the father of a great nation through which all the families of the earth would be blessed. Oh, you should have heard him! His eyes would gaze far off into the distance and reflect the fire light, as if his eyes had become fiery suns blazing in the heaven of his dream. Then he'd look at me, scorching me with his intensity, and say, ''So you can see, my son, how important your birth was to us. We'd almost given up on God's promise when you were conceived.'' Then he'd rub his whiskers and mutter almost to himself, ''That conception was God's doing, not mine.'' The way he said it, I wasn't sure whether he meant he was proud or resentful.

Anyway, it all felt very heavy to me: all his words about the promise and being a great nation, and the unmistakable implication that I was supposed to do something about it; the inference, pervasive as incense, that everything about that old man's life came down on my shoulders, depended on me. To be honest, part of me preened in the glow of being that important. But another, larger part of me resented the pressure as smotheringly oppressive, even as perhaps a part of my father, unacknowledged by him, resented God putting so much on him. Besides, I really didn't believe it was all up to me. But I did delight in the feeling of being alive. I was grateful for my life, however it had happened. So, along with my resentment, I was glad for that hundred-year-old Billy Goat.

In spite of his intensity and solemnity, I'd laugh at things my father took with dead seriousness, and I'd laugh at him. My father would say, "You are well named, my son." And I'd say, "Why, father?" I knew his answer, but I hoped he'd tell it differently sometime. He never did. Each time he'd say, "Isaac means 'He laughs.' When God told us you were to be born, your mother and I laughed. We were so old, we didn't think it possible to have a child. God must have been angry at our laughter, for he told me then to name you Isaac. He meant your name as a rebuke to us."

My father never deviated from that version of the story. Even as a boy, I thought he'd missed the point of my name and what it meant. But after while, his story helped me understand a little of why my laughter made him so angry. What I didn't understand was why he never caught on to what I thought was the larger joke, the joke that made me keep laughing. His mind was made up.

Then I started wondering if maybe I was missing something after all. Maybe I was the one who didn't get the point of what was going on. He was my father, after all—this stubborn, stiff, upright man who asked so much of me. Maybe he was right about me . . . and about God. I was confused. How could I please this man with whom I felt so competitive? How could I get close to this man who seemed to squeeze the breath out of me whenever I was around him? I wanted him to laugh with me, or even laugh *at* me, because laughter was in me. But when he didn't laugh—wouldn't laugh— maybe I laughed just to cover my confusion, my disappointment at his disappointment. I don't know.

Then one day, when I was about fourteen, my father took me hunting for the first time. He thought he'd teach me how to shoot the bow. How stupid he was! By the time I was fourteen, I'd been hunting with friends for years. But he didn't know because he'd been so busy with his own business. On that day he explained everything to me and shot an arrow or two himself. He missed the target, the tree, missed everything. Then I took the bow and, quicker than I can tell you about it, shot three arrows into a space on a tree as small as a rabbit's head. He was shocked, and he began to fume at me. I laughed before I smelled the smoke of him.

I thought he'd be proud. I didn't understand the depth or the threat of our competition. I didn't understand that there could be murder in a father's heart, or in a son's heart. I don't think he understood it either, but as the spit of that moment turned slowly over our encounter, smoke from the fire of our murderous fantasies suddenly stung our eyes and our souls to tears. I realized I was afraid of my father, afraid for my father. I don't think either of us wanted to admit that there was murder between us. Nor were we able to trust that our love went as deep as our rage and fear, or deeper. Now I wonder if my own sons trust that.

Brash with youth as I was then, I leaned on the bow and started telling my father about bits of my plans. Well, actually, they weren't exactly plans; they were more like dreams, vague desires, the oats of a young man that I knew would get his goat—or his attention—and maybe get our differences, and similarities, out in the open so we might see and understand them a little. Now, I think I just wanted to feel important to *him*, not just to his damned dream. I was groping to understand why I loved my father and hated him at the same time, why I wanted to be close to him and yet to escape him.

So, I started by saying, ''Well, you Old Billy Goat, now that you know I am strong and can shoot a bow better than almost anyone, maybe you'll agree that it's time I joined Ishmael in the wilderness and became a hunter for the rest of my life. Or maybe you'll think about helping set me up to make bows and sell them, and teach people how to shoot. Maybe you'll give me some contacts back in Ur where I could really be a success at it. What do you think?''

He started stammering, "You can't . . . you can't do that . . . you're my . . . dream . . . a great nation . . . God's promise?''

I replied, "Oh, quit bahing. All that is *your* business, you Old Goat, not mine. I don't even understand what any of it means, or what

I have to do with it. I'm me, and I'd rather be a hunter.'' I laughed and looked squarely in his eyes.

It was true. I didn't know what all his talk about God's promise to make him a great nation really meant. All that came through to me was that I had to be just like him, do just what he did (or what he thought I should do), carry out some grand plan he'd drawn up . . . or that he and God had drawn up, however that might have happened.

He and God—that was the heart of it! Trace the plan back far enough, and Abraham's dreams were all mixed up with God's demands. How could that be? How could Abraham be so sure what I was supposed to do? But with God on his side, I had no effective way to resist. It all seemed so unjust to me. Was God unjust? After all, God hadn't spoken to me. Besides, what is a great nation, anyway? Abraham's ideas about it didn't sound so great to me. There was no room for enjoyment and laughter in it. And if there was no laughter in it, what was so appealing about it? And why was I named Isaac? Why had God given me that name? I started to raise those questions with Abraham, but somehow my thoughts tumbled past the control of words. So I turned to retrieve the arrows.

I kept laughing as I walked away, and I hadn't gone twenty paces when something hit a glancing blow on the back of my shoulder. I whirled and looked back. My father had thrown his hunting spear at me! In a flash I put an arrow in my bow and aimed it at him. He didn't flinch. He was a tough old goat. We stared at each other—father and son!

In that moment I thought a thousand thoughts. My father was a hundred years old when I was born. I was not an unmixed blessing to him, but he couldn't admit that to anyone, especially to himself. He was such a stubborn man, defeated by his own victories. I had not turned out to be the audience he'd hoped for, an audience to applaud his achievements. I was not even the product of his own potencies, which he might have seen as a blessing if he'd looked at it that way. After all, seeing their children as a product—and therefore a possession—of their own potencies is a destructive illusion, an illusion which most parents are never stripped of, and, therefore, many children are damaged by. I was obviously a *gift* to him, given to him. My life had emerged out of his almost death, but he resented that rather than rejoiced in it.

So, I reminded my father of his impotency when it was his *potency* he wanted more than anything, a potency confirmed and fulfilled by a son of his own. HIS VERY OWN! A son to carry on his work. A son to build a monument to him, the father. But I had laughed, and he had hurled his spear. He wanted his potencies just as I, at that moment, wanted mine.

I lowered my bow and laughed again. We were fools, such fools. The joke was on us. What Abraham wanted was for me—and God—to meet his terms. The issue was power. All those years he had wanted, actually had expected, God to force me to conform to his own dream. But I hadn't. Why? Why hadn't I? That was his question. Was it God, or me, or him who had failed? Sadly, his life had come down to a failure to be explained, or blamed, or changed. For me, the issues were different: I struggled to understand why my *not* conforming to his dream should be considered a failure in the first place.

In that moment I knew there had to be a test—a test for me as well as for Abraham. As I moved toward him, he spun and started home without a word—a jerky, stiff-legged old goat. I followed him. Love and murder and the urgent question hung in the air behind us: Who had failed whom, and why?

The next morning we started out on our journey to Moriah. Neither of us knew exactly what to expect or how to arrange things. You must remember that I was only fourteen, strong and full of myself, but not as sure of things as I acted. I had no idea what the test would be . . . perhaps some kind of reading of the entrails of a bird, of a lamb maybe, a discerning of signs in the appearance of the animal's organs, and then a burnt offering to God. Some of the neighboring tribes used children instead of animals for that kind of sacrifice, but not us . . . not yet!

Two servants went with us, and an ass, but for some reason, it was important to father that I carry the wood and he carry the fire in a small brazier. When I asked him about the sacrifice, he only said grimly, ''God will provide the sacrifice.'' So I sweat under my load of wood, muttering my resentments under my breath: ''Young beast . . . young beast . . . young beast!'' And under my resentments was the ache of fear and yet the throb of anticipation. I knew it was no ordinary thing we were about that day, or the following two days it took to reach our destination.

I watched my father as we climbed. He wanted to prove something. But to whom? To me? To God? To himself? It began to dawn on me that he actually *would* sacrifice me to prove whatever it was. His obsession had driven him from murderous fantasies to righteous sacrifices. He was like a goat butting his way up that mountain, butting against the frustrated dream he was trapped in. He would force God to open the goat pen. As for me, I knew nothing would ever again be the same for either of us, however this came out.

I also knew, in some dim way I couldn't have explained, that I was trying to prove something as well. I, too, was testing the God whom my father seemed to know so well. I just could not believe God had given me my name without reason. I couldn't believe that human beings were to be sacrificed to God's demands. I couldn't believe that God would confirm my father's dream, confirm that I was doomed to hunt my father's prey because we are doomed, finally, to act out some terrible drama of God's compulsions. If that was the way of it, I decided death was preferable! If that was the way of it, then my father and I were both the butt of a joke. I had to find out. Was my laughter the mere bleating of a lamb on the way to the slaughter, or was it the language of God, the music of love? Was my laughter the sound of despair or freedom? I climbed on beside my father.

Everything on that climb seemed to happen so slowly. Birds hung motionless in the air, their wings not beating against the sky. A falling leaf never drifted to the ground. The sun stood immobile as a hunter waiting for his prey. A mountain stream parted silently on a rock, the splintered shards of water forever scattered toward the sky. My heart beat once, stopped, and the rest was echo.

Then we were there, alone on the mountain top. I looked at my father; I saw tears in his eyes, and a fierce determination. His mind, his heart were fixed. All his years were gathered in that moment, that place. And all mine. I laughed sharply, once, but it was quickly sheathed in the wind. My father turned away. My laughter went inside, muted into watchful hope.

I was afraid, and tears trickled down my face as we built the altar and laid the wood, both of us waiting for something we couldn't name. Even more slowly, he tied my hands and feet, not looking at me. I did not resist. The test had to be. Was he waiting for me to scream for him to stop, to cry for mercy and swear that I would do what he wanted and never laugh again? Surely not. I couldn't, wouldn't do that! The travesty of the expectation made me laugh inside! What would it possibly mean to him to force me like that? It would be a farce! A mockery!

And me, what was I waiting for? For him to confess his stubbornness, to recant his dream, to acknowledge that his life, his faith had been lived in error, for nothing? But I didn't want his life. I wanted mine. Yet for either of us to win now, at the expense of the other, would only perpetuate the tyranny, only complete the imprisonment of each of us in the other's life. We were both trapped, perhaps always had been. In that moment it seemed that we were the butt of each other's joke: one murdering to prove something, the other allowing the murder in order to murder back, and so to prove something. Our minds were set, and what we seemed to be proving was that we were fools, fools whose lives meant nothing, fools who were, in truth, the butt of God's joke.

Straining and sweating, Abraham lifted me onto the altar. As best I could, I helped him. Then he reached for his knife and raised it high and held it waiting, waiting. I looked at his face, and I saw the tears and the despair and the awful, unbending pride.

"Look at me," I wanted to scream, "*look* at me." The words wouldn't come. My mouth was dry. His eyes were toward the heavens. At last I had become only a thing to be done, a challenge to be hurled at God, a prayer to be offered to a mocking void, a sacrifice to some eternal, unchanging, uncaring order. At that moment it seemed my father's fanaticism would prevail. My life would be sacrificed to his dream, and his life sacrificed to what he perceived to be God's dream. There would be no breaking the cycle!

When you are about to die, when disaster is about to overwhelm you, what do you do? I searched for something to fasten my eyes on, something so real and solid that it wouldn't disappear, thinking maybe if I could hold on, even with my eyes, I wouldn't disappear. Dimly I could hear my father uttering a prayer. I lifted my head a little so I could see around me. I told myself, "Look, look hard, look ... there ... a tree, a rock, the thunderheads, a storm moving in. Concentrate on that and ..."

And then I saw it. Later, my father said it was a ram. Maybe it was, but it looked like a goat to me. Usually goats high in the mountain are agile, quick-footed and sure. But this one was stumbling and staggering down the path like he'd had too much wine, or was tired from dancing all night, or was just old and stiff, like my father. I was about to yell something when an enormous bolt of lightning cut through the sky, and a clap of thunder rolled and echoed from mountain to mountain.

The flash and roar frightened the goat, and he jumped and skittered and stumbled into a thicket of vetch and vine rose. He tottered drunkenly and apparently caught his balance only to discover that his horns were tangled in the vines. That made him furious. He started thrashing and butting and struggling, raising an awful ruckus. I started to laugh, and the more the old goat butted and thrashed, the harder I laughed.

I looked up at my father. He still had his arms upraised, but his eyes were on that goat, and his mouth was wide open. His beard was swaying gently in the breeze. When I looked back at the old goat in the vines, its mouth was open, too, panting, and its beard was swaying in the breeze. They were so alike! I laughed so hard I fell off the altar.

When I managed to sit up, I heard my father chuckling a little, and I said, gasping for air, "That old goat ... over there ... looks just like you."

Abraham looked down at me and actually started laughing, laughing for the first time I could ever remember, laughing in little spurts and coughs like he wasn't used to it, but couldn't stop either. He choked out, "I was about to say he looks like you—stupid and young."

I managed to sputter, "I hadn't thought of that, but maybe you're right." As I pictured myself as a goat, I laughed all the harder.

There we were, my father and I, laughing together while the storm was breaking, the rain beginning to pour down on us, the goat still thrashing like a tippler in the thicket. It was almost too obvious a comic epiphany. If another moment had passed, if the thunder hadn't rolled, the knife might have plunged and my laughter been forever cut short. Instead, the laughter came like the deep breath of a reprieve which the hunter—and surely the hunted—takes when the arrow misses (something I strangely have often wanted to happen, even as I have drawn and released the arrow). For me, this moment, the laughter of it, was life out of death, the sound of a flute on a starless night. Surely it was reminiscent of the time God told my parents I was on the way, and they laughed.

When we had stopped laughing quite so hard, Abraham pointed to the goat and chortled, "He does look a little like me, doesn't he?"

I giggled, "And like me."

Finally Abraham composed himself and ventured, rather solemnly, "I think God has spoken to us."

"Yes," I nodded, eagerly anticipating what this discovery would mean to us.

Abraham went on: "We must not let our laughter profane the sacredness of what has happened, or obscure the message."

I was bewildered. "Obscure? Father, don't you think the laughter *is* the message?"

"No," he insisted, "no! In the thunder and the lightning, God spoke to us. I have been vindicated. I have met the test and proven I am faithful and God-fearing. God has provided the ram over there as a sacrifice to seal the promise He has renewed to me."

Amazing! At that moment I didn't know what to say to my father, that blind old goat of a man. So I rested my head on his leg and said, as gently as I could, "Father, you Old Goat, did it ever occur to you that you aren't the only one God renewed a promise to? What about me?"

He seemed genuinely surprised. "You?"

"Yes, me," I insisted. "Do you suppose it's possible that maybe God didn't really speak in the thunder and the lightning, that maybe you're missing the point?"

Well, that did it. Abraham turned bright red, his mouth clenched so tightly it looked like a knife slit through the fur of his beard, while his eyes flared and took over his face. He began to fumble around for his knife, his hands shaking so badly he couldn't seem to pick it up. But strangely I felt more frustrated than frightened. In the past I would have taunted him more, or walked away, but this time I felt like there might be a chance for something different to happen, and I didn't want to lose it.

So as calmly, yet as rapidly as I could, I said, "Wait a minute, father. Listen to me, please! You said God told you to name me Isaac, and all these years you thought my name was God's *rebuke* to you for laughing at the impossibility of my being born when you and mother were so old. But maybe it wasn't a rebuke at all. Maybe it was a wonderful joke, a cause for laughter, a reminder that laughter is good. Just now, when we laughed together, I felt closer to you than I ever had. Wasn't our laughing together wonderful? Wasn't it?"

Abraham stopped fumbling for his knife, and his face relaxed a bit into a quizzical look. "Laughter is frivolous," he countered warily.

I pressed my point. "Father, did you ever think that maybe too much seriousness is frivolous?"

Abraham was uncompromising. "No!" he insisted. "You are wrong. We must be serious with God. It is the only way."

I laughed. "The *only* way, father? Just as having children when you are young is the only way to have them?"

Suddenly his eyes filled with tears and his shoulders sagged, then shrugged. He seemed so defenseless. He whispered hoarsely, "I've tried to do the right thing all my life."

I wasn't sure how to respond, and I squirmed, aware of how uncomfortable I was, sitting on the wet ground, my hands and feet tied. "Could you please cut me free, father?" I asked. Without using the knife, or looking directly in my eyes, Abraham managed to undo the ropes.

I stood and rubbed my wrists. He had turned away and was looking out over the distant valley. I went over and put my hand on his shoulder. "Father, I know you have always tried to do the right thing. I respect you for that. It's just that . . ." I groped after the words.

He turned toward me slightly and said very softly, "It's just that, what?"

I took a deep breath and plunged ahead. "Well, it's just that there isn't only one way to do things, one way it has to be ... for everyone. Even for you. Or me. Maybe impossibility is *our* word, father, not God's word. Maybe that's what laughter is about, to remind us of many different possibilities. Maybe God wanted me named Isaac because God was laughing at the preposterous thing He was doing."

Abraham turned full toward me, his face a battleground of conflicting responses: disbelief, curiosity, anger, longing. "God laughing?" I could see him rolling the image over in his mind. "It doesn't seem possible," he said slowly, but in such a way that didn't dismiss the possibility of it.

"Neither did my birth," I chuckled, "but here I am. Father, doesn't it occur to you that God threw laughter into us, just like He threw the rainbow into the heavens, because laughter is a sign of the joy of life and all the things God makes possible in it? Couldn't it be that because we could laugh at ourselves just now, we might find a different way to be father and son than we've ever been before? I think we should laugh at ourselves because we are such fools, with all our arguing about the way it *has* to be for us."

Abraham listened carefully, and for a long moment he was silent. Then, in a solemn voice which cracked with what I sensed was a smile, he said, "I am not a fool. I may look like a goat, but I am not one."

I risked laughing aloud. "But, father, you are very much like that old goat over there, and so am I. We've been so tangled up in our ingrown virtues and certainties that we've left God out. Maybe what happened just now is God's way of reminding us that our lives don't have to be that way, reminding us that we can change them."

Just about then, the goat in the thicket got a second wind and started jumping up and down, trying to butt himself out of the vines in a burst of terrible frenzy. In what sounded like a burst of relief of something pent up for a long, long time, Abraham started laughing. Then, more freely than I had ever laughed with anyone,

I joined the laughter. After what seemed forever, after we had laughed ourselves into a kind of easy, peaceful tiredness, my father and I sat together and leaned against the altar we had built.

I said, "Father, I think maybe that goat really is what God is trying to say to us, a kind of offering from God to us."

Abraham put his head back against the stones, gazed at the sun spilling a thousand radiant streams through holes in the dike of the clouds, and replied warily, yet almost tenderly, "Offering, my son? What are you saying now?"

I looked at this old man next to me, watched the sunlight glisten on his forehead, the wind ruffle wisps of his hair in what seemed the gentle way of a lover, and I wanted just to touch him. I dared to take one of his fingers lightly in my hand and said, "I'm just saying that maybe God is willing to be the butt of the joke in order for us to change our ways and be free. You had a dream, father, and I am what you got. So here we are, a couple of human beings who can laugh together at ourselves, maybe even laugh with God, and maybe help each other live this amazing life a little differently. I guess God made us gifts to each other. Maybe that's not only the way of it, but the miracle of it. Do you think we can learn to fight and play and build and still keep from killing each other with our knives and our dreams?"

I watched his face intently. He closed his eyes, and I think he nodded his head ever so slightly, though it could have been the wind. Then, sounding disappointingly like the croak of a raven, the words came from my suddenly dry mouth: "I love you, Old Goat." I felt his body shudder slightly, as if at the end of a sob. Then he did the most amazing thing. He began to laugh very softly, and he took my hand in his and held it against his heart. I began to laugh, too, and put my head on his shoulder. After a time, we grew quiet and wordlessly watched the darkness creep across the sky and the stars appear in their reassuring clusters.

Things had begun to change for my father and me, up there on that mountain. Still, I found myself wondering then, as I do now, if fathers and sons, parents and children, and children's children will ever really learn not to kill each other with their weapons and dreams. I wonder if we'll ever really learn how amazing we are, and life is, and God is. If we do, maybe the only way we'll really die is laughing, and our dying will be into life. In any case, I'm glad for my life and my name Isaac.

(Genesis 17, 22;
Matthew 1:1–18, especially verse 2)

BREAKING UP

SARAH: You are un-be-lievable, Abraham! I've just about had it with you! Why didn't you tell me where you were going and what you were planning when you went off like that?

ABRAHAM: Because I wasn't sure. And I didn't have a plan, exactly.

SARAH: What do you mean, you didn't have a plan? You come back here and tell me you went on a three day trip, took along all that wood and fire, climbed a mountain, almost sacrificed Isaac to God, and you have the brass to stand there and tell me it wasn't *planned*? It wasn't exactly a stroll in the meadow, Abraham. Why? What stupid reason could you possibly have for doing such an absurd thing?

ABRAHAM: Stop it! Stop jabbering like a jackdaw and listen, Sarah! I'm trying to tell you what happened because I'm not sure I can explain it. That's why I need to talk about it now.

SARAH: *Afterward*, you want to talk!

ABRAHAM: Yes! Maybe you can help me. Because something happened that I don't understand. Before this, I thought it was just between Isaac and me.

SARAH: Abraham, I am his mother! What do you think

that means? His *mother*! You go off to kill Isaac
to settle some male thing, and I am not involved?
It is not between *us*? Has age scrambled your
senses? Why didn't you talk to me about it *before*
you went? Why?

ABRAHAM: Because I knew you'd try to talk me out of it and
I didn't want to argue.

SARAH: Of course I would have tried to talk you out of
it. I would have done anything to stop you. Do
you hear me? Anything!

ABRAHAM: Look, try to understand, will you? It was
something I had to do, something between God
and me. I heard God's voice telling me to sacrifice Isaac.

SARAH: Why didn't I hear anything? Isaac isn't just *your*
son. Why didn't you ask me if I heard God's
voice?

ABRAHAM: Because I knew you hadn't. You would have protested, argued with me.

SARAH: Why didn't *you* protest?

ABRAHAM: Because it was God's voice.

SARAH: No! Oh no! If you had been so sure it was God's
voice, you would have told me before you went
off to kill Isaac. You were afraid to tell me because
you *weren't* sure.

ABRAHAM: That's not so! I just didn't want to argue, and I
knew you would have tried to talk me out of it.

SARAH: Yes! Yes, I would have, and I'll tell you why: the
voice I hear would be different. It would say . . .
it *said* . . . your plan to sacrifice Isaac was wrong.
Absurd! Stupid! Even you know that, now,
because you didn't go through with it.

ABRAHAM: You heard God's voice?

SARAH: Yes. Well, not exactly. I don't know. I just know
God's voice would be different from what you
heard.

ABRAHAM: How do you know?

SARAH:	How does *anyone* know? Isn't that really the problem here? Isn't that what you're trying to figure out? How *does* anyone know?
ABRAHAM:	Okay. Then are we so different? When God told you we would have a child, you laughed. You didn't believe it.
SARAH:	No, I didn't. All the signs that I could have children had long since stopped. Of course I laughed. So did you!
ABRAHAM:	I didn't think it was possible either after all those years. Once I'd heard God's voice clearly promising to make my name great, make a great nation of me. But it had long since seemed too late for any of that to happen. I'd gambled so much on that promise. I wanted to do so much, be so much. And it wasn't happening. I laughed because I didn't think it could happen. My laugh was scornful. I'd *never* have a great name.
SARAH:	We were so ambitious, weren't we? We wanted to make such a name for ourselves. Now Isaac is our only chance. Why, *why* did you want to kill him?
ABRAHAM:	That's just it, Sarah, I don't know. We're getting so old. And after all these years we only have one son. One! It's laughable. All this time, all this effort, and my name still isn't great. We'll never be a great nation now. None of it will ever happen. Maybe it was despair that drove me to go up that mountain.
SARAH:	You always wanted so much.
ABRAHAM:	So did you. You just said *we* were ambitious, both of us.
SARAH:	I suppose.
ABRAHAM:	Do you remember when we left Haran to go out and make a name for ourselves?
SARAH:	Yes, I was beautiful then, not scrawny and wrinkled.

ABRAHAM: And why we left the security of our home and families? Do you remember why?

SARAH: We left because everything had stopped. Everyone knew how music should sound—all brass and drums—and that was it. If you wanted to add a flute or harp, it wasn't considered music.

ABRAHAM: It was that way for poetry, too. Just so many stanzas, a definite rhythm, no deviation. And it was that way for religion. A different god assigned to every area of life. Everyone knew how the gods behaved and what it took to please them. I kept asking, "What if there is only one God?" And the priests would answer, "There are too many contradictions in life. Only one God could not account for them all." "Maybe God is complicated," I would argue. They threatened to kill me for challenging the truth of their many gods.

SARAH: Just as you threatened to kill Isaac?

ABRAHAM: Strange that you say that. I thought the same thing on the way down from the mountain. I gagged on the idea. Am I no different from those priests?

SARAH: Yes, you are different, but maybe not so different as you'd like to think. Is it important to be so different, Abraham?

ABRAHAM: I'm not sure. Maybe it is. You wanted to be different from Hagar! You arranged for me to have a child with her when she was your maid. And then, after she had Ishmael, you forced me to throw her out, send her into the desert to die.

SARAH: So what? What does that prove? That we're even? That we're both wrong? What is so important about our being different? It's a curse.

ABRAHAM: But isn't that why we left Haran? Remember the excitement of it? It was going to be such an adventure. We were going to do such great things. We were going to be different, remember?

SARAH: I don't remember it that way. I think the truth is that we wanted to be *better* than the people we were leaving behind.

ABRAHAM: No! No, that wasn't it.

SARAH: No? Why this sudden squeamishness? Why dress the truth in silky words that rustle of lies? Faith's not served by deceit. Of course we wanted to be better than other people. That's honestly what it was all about, wasn't it: being a great nation? having a great name? At least that's what sold me then. I think we took a big risk, and we wanted credit for it. Everyone wants credit, more and more credit. Admit it! And when we don't get credit, we give blame. You, me, everyone. Come on, own up to it! If despair drove you to go up that mountain to kill Isaac, it wasn't the despair of not being different. It was the despair of not getting credit, not having a great name. That's your male obsession.

ABRAHAM: Is it really? Who gave you the right to pass judgment? You dump your female garbage on me and then complain that I stink! Come on, yourself! Why were *you* in such despair when you were childless and Ishmael was my only heir? I'll tell you: it was because you wouldn't get the credit you wanted. It would all go to Hagar as Ishmael's mother, and you couldn't stand that.

SARAH: All right, all right! I'll admit that credit isn't just a male issue. But it sure seems like it is because you get so much more of it. So it's an issue for both of us. All right! Now, can you see that if you'd killed Isaac, I'd have lost the only thing I ever did, the only thing I might get credit for? Maybe you are right, Abraham: you and I are not so different after all.

ABRAHAM: But don't you see? That's the point. Neither of us gets *any* credit for having Isaac! We were so old, his birth was almost a mockery of us.

SARAH: Is that why you wanted to kill him?

ABRAHAM: Will you listen? I keep telling you, I don't think I *wanted* to kill him. That's what I don't understand. Maybe I *was* angry at God because Isaac was the only heir I had. And not only that, he was so different from what I expected and wanted. It had all seemed so possible when we were young—having a great name, being a great nation.

SARAH: Yes, it did. Until all that time went by.

ABRAHAM: Only one son. For a long time I've felt like such a failure. Everything's so cursedly fragile. It's almost as if I've never even been here, on this earth. My life is like dust in the wind.

SARAH: You did have great dreams.

ABRAHAM: It wasn't just a dream. It was God's promise, Sarah.

SARAH: That's what *you* said. But the promise always sounded to me like your dreams.

ABRAHAM: I don't know. Maybe you're right. Maybe that's the trouble. You know what came to me up on the mountain, Sarah?

SARAH: What?

ABRAHAM: I realized that I wasn't able to tell the difference between my dreams and God's voice anymore.

SARAH: Were you ever able to tell the difference very clearly?

ABRAHAM: I thought so. You know what it is to have a dream. Is it so hard to tell the difference between the voice of dreams and the voice of God?

SARAH: I never was able to have my own dreams. It must be nice to dream.

ABRAHAM: But you did dream! You shared the dream, too, when you set out with me from Haran.

SARAH: But, it was still *your* dream. Besides, you said it was God's voice.

ABRAHAM: I thought it was. I was *sure* it was.

SARAH: Maybe you are wiser now for realizing that your dreams and God's promises might be different.

ABRAHAM:	Maybe. But I didn't realize the difference when I started up that mountain with Isaac. All I knew was that my dream wasn't coming true, that it would never happen the way I wanted. Sarah, I've been wondering. It sounds crazy, but . . . do you suppose maybe we try to kill what we think isn't possible for us?
SARAH:	Kill it? You mean just get rid of it, deny it?
ABRAHAM:	Yes.
SARAH:	Why? Because what we think isn't possible torments us? Is that what you think?
ABRAHAM:	Something like that. Yes.
SARAH:	Maybe. Or maybe it's more likely that we try to kill what we can't make happen and take credit for. So you tried to kill Isaac, and I tried to kill Ishmael. God have mercy, what kind of monsters are we? Oh, Abraham, it's awful to be old and look back.
ABRAHAM:	Yes, I was thinking the same thing. And then it occurred to me that our past and our dreams haven't killed us yet. You'd think they would have, but they haven't. It dawned on me coming down the mountain: we are still here, Sarah— you, me, Isaac, and even Ishmael. I'm not sure why, but we are. That's what I'm hanging on to right now.
SARAH:	You're right. We *are* still here, old as we are. That's amazing, isn't it? Who can figure it out? You would think we'd have done ourselves in by now. But, no! I wonder why not. Maybe something just wouldn't let us.
ABRAHAM:	In spite of all the times we mucked it all up.
SARAH:	Do you remember the time we strayed into Egypt after leaving Haran? And you told the Pharaoh I was your sister? That was a betrayal of me, Abraham. I never said so before, but it was.
ABRAHAM:	Betrayal? What do you mean? I did it to save our lives, Sarah!

SARAH: You did it to save *your* life, Abraham. You were afraid to tell the Pharaoh I was your wife because I was beautiful, and you were sure he would kill you in order to have me. So I had to pretend to be your sister and sleep with him in order to save you. It was ugly, dirty, a terrible humiliation. I still feel the humiliation, and the rage!

ABRAHAM: But you agreed to it beforehand!

SARAH: I agreed because you said I had to! You were so obsessed with your foolish dream you couldn't see anything else.

ABRAHAM: That's not so! Suppose I had told the Pharaoh you were my wife! Would you have let him kill me in order to save your *own* life? Of course you would have! Don't lie.

SARAH: I don't know if I would have. Maybe. Probably. Maybe in some dim way I realized that if it was the other way around, I might have saved myself at your expense. I suppose that's why I could do what I did: sleep with him, do the whole rotten thing. I don't know. But the point is that it was still a terrible humiliation. It was like a rape. A rape, Abraham! Do you know that?

ABRAHAM: I know, I know. It was humiliating for me, too—feeling impotent. I was ashamed. I wanted to run away. For me it was a rape of the heart.

SARAH: I know. I think I knew that even then. But you didn't run. If you had, it would have been a total betrayal. And I didn't run either. So, as you said, we're still here.

ABRAHAM: There's been a lot of competition between us, hasn't there?

SARAH: Maybe. I guess it was hidden, mostly, but, yes, I felt it.

ABRAHAM: To me it felt like we were in a struggle for power.

SARAH: Power? I never had any power. *You* had all the power.

ABRAHAM:	Wrong! You *do* have power. It's just as great as mine. It may be less obvious, but it's just as great. Why do you deny it?
SARAH:	What power?
ABRAHAM:	Beauty. Brains. Sex. Seduction. Motherhood. You controlled Isaac from the time he was born.
SARAH:	Only because you abandoned him to me. You were busy, totally absorbed in your dreams.
ABRAHAM:	That's your excuse. Did it ever occur to you that I was absorbed in my dream because you took Isaac from me? You made alliances with him as he grew, and somehow you conspired to portray me as the enemy. The truth is that you bound him to you as surely as I bound his hands and feet when I was about to sacrifice him on the mountain.
SARAH:	He was all I had.
ABRAHAM:	What else did you want? Whatever it was, you never told me. You never confronted me with anything about abandonment. Why? Because you reveled in the power you had over Isaac! And over me!
SARAH:	That's not true! You never challenged our so-called "alliance." You never tried to get close to Isaac. Don't blame me for that. Besides, I never had any power over you.
ABRAHAM:	Sarah, surely you're not blind. Or stupid. Why do you think I was so absorbed in my dreams?
SARAH:	Who knows? It was for your own twisted reasons. It was for yourself!
ABRAHAM:	Yes, it was for me, but it was more than that. What else did I have? Besides, Isaac was *not* all you had: you had me, and you know it. Don't pull that innocent, powerless act on me; it won't work. I was raised by a woman, too, you know. I learned. So let's be honest. Ridiculous as it may seem, I was always a little afraid of you, more than a

little. I wanted your favor and never felt I could get it. Not really. I wanted you to think I was attractive. I wanted you to be excited sexually about me. I was forever trying to please you, get your approval. That was also what my dreams were about. And you knew it! You knew all that about me and weren't above using it for your own gain.

SARAH: So, finally, we're coming out of hiding, are we? Well, you're right, I did know you and how to get you to do things. And I did benefit in some ways from that, but I never thought of it as having power. And I never really saw you as someone less than powerful, until today. If you wanted to know, why didn't you ask me what I really wanted instead of assuming you knew and just blindly trying to please me? Why didn't you talk to me, *listen* to me? Why didn't you tell me about your fears, and struggles? I would have listened. Gladly!

ABRAHAM: It just seemed too hard.

SARAH: It was easier for you to drag Isaac up that mountain to kill him?

ABRAHAM: Was it easier for you to drive Ishmael and Hagar away than to deal with me about your jealousy or insecurity? Was it easier for you to bind Isaac to you than to tell me directly what you really wanted for yourself?

SARAH: Maybe it was, I don't know. All right, sure it was. It must have been easier, for both of us. But you're right, we're still here. And it is amazing that our past and our dreams haven't killed us yet! Something must keep us from doing ourselves in, keep giving us another chance.

ABRAHAM: Sarah, that's just what I've been trying to figure out. All the way up the mountain, I kept trying to sort out the difference between the voice of God and my own dreams. And I couldn't do it! That scared me.

SARAH: Did you ever think maybe they overlap? After all, God gave us the ability to dream! Maybe dreams are just a third ear, cocked a little toward God.

ABRAHAM: But there has to be some difference between dreams and God's voice, Sarah. When Isaac was on the altar and the knife was in my hand, I looked into his eyes, and then I looked toward the heavens for a sign. There wasn't any sign there. There was nothing but wind and clouds and this little gopher of a thought that kept scurrying around in my head, clawing its way into my mind from somewhere down inside me.

SARAH: What thought?

ABRAHAM: It wasn't a thought so much as a question. Who was I *really* killing? Isaac, because he wasn't as perfect as my dream wanted him to be? But then I realized that if he *was* that perfect, he wouldn't be human. And he certainly wouldn't be Isaac. In fact, if he had managed to be that perfect, it would mean I'd already killed him in every way that matters because I would have forced him to do things the way I thought they should be, do what I could not do or be myself.

SARAH: Thank God for gopher thoughts.

ABRAHAM: But the questioning went on, Sarah. I began wondering if in some way I was killing you by taking Isaac away from you because *you* weren't as perfect as my dream either. I was shocked at how perverse I would be to sacrifice Isaac to hurt you. And I realized I didn't really want to hurt you. So then I began asking if actually I was killing myself because I wasn't as perfect as my dream demanded of me, or as perfect as I pretended to be— even if you and I really knew I wasn't.

SARAH: Oh, Abraham, I never realized you were so tormented.

ABRAHAM: Then the question became, did God actually demand such perfection of me when I saw it was inhuman to demand it of Isaac? And I thought, no, probably God didn't demand that. So I asked myself, why not stop pretending? Why kill anyone for a fraud? Why not just confess it? Was my pride going to make me a killer? And then I realized I really don't have much to be proud of anyway. That's when I dropped the knife, Sarah!

SARAH: Oh, Abraham, maybe those questions are part of a new dream. I think you have more to be proud of than you realize.

ABRAHAM: You mean because I dropped the knife?

SARAH: Yes, that. And more than that, because you heard the questions, paid attention to them. Don't you think they might have been the voice of God?

ABRAHAM: But the questions didn't come from outside; they came from inside. The voice asking the questions was inside me. I didn't hear it with my ears. I heard it with my heart, my mind.

SARAH: Why couldn't God's voice come that way?

ABRAHAM: Because it's different from the way it came before.

SARAH: Suppose it was different. Does that mean it wasn't God? Just because you heard the voice outside before doesn't mean that's the only way. For me, the voice was always inside, only I never thought to call it the voice of God. Until now. Abraham, we have to help each other listen. We have to talk to each other. We have to talk about our different voices.

ABRAHAM: Different voices? You sound like the priests in Haran. God doesn't speak in different voices, Sarah!

SARAH: Are you so sure? Abraham, listen! Maybe there's another way to see this. Maybe God isn't just outside us, or inside us, but *between* us.

ABRAHAM: Between us?

SARAH:	Yes, between us.
ABRAHAM:	I don't understand what you mean!
SARAH:	Between us, in our talking, in helping each other see something either of us alone might have missed.
ABRAHAM:	I don't know. It sounds ... possible, I guess. I'm not sure.
SARAH:	Look, Abraham. Isn't loving between us?
ABRAHAM:	I never thought about it. Yes, I suppose love is between us. So?
SARAH:	So, couldn't God's love be in our love? And don't you suppose our trusting God might come in our learning to trust each other?
ABRAHAM:	Maybe. It seems right, anyway. I suppose if God's love isn't in our love, it wouldn't matter much, would it? I never thought of it that way. Oh, Sarah, think of the chances I've missed.
SARAH:	Yes, but think of the chances we still *have* as long as we're still here!
ABRAHAM:	Maybe so. But ... Sarah, I have something else to tell you. Afterward, after I dropped the knife, Isaac and I sat together, and we laughed a little. Can you imagine? We actually laughed together. And through the tears in my eyes, I watched the rays of the sun gently rub the back of the earth as with a thousand fingers. Then one possible difference between my dreams and God's voice came to me.
SARAH:	What was it?
ABRAHAM:	Well, at first my dreams seemed so attractive, so achievable. But sooner or later they almost killed me and you and Isaac, and everybody around me. On the other hand, at first God's voice seems hard, but sooner or later it leads to life. At least I believe it does. But I got confused, you know, because the idea of sacrificing Isaac was *so* hard, so awfully hard, I thought it came from God. It

must have, just because it was hard. Stupid, isn't it, to think that way! Well, I was ... wrong. Now, I wonder if the way to tell the difference between our dreams and God's voice isn't to try to figure out what leads to life and what leads to death.

SARAH: Yes, I think so, too. And I think what you're really talking about is the difference between what you hear with your third ear, and what's only your own voice or the babble of everyone else.

ABRAHAM: But that's just it, Sarah. Before, God just *told* us what to do.

SARAH: Maybe that's what is hard about hearing God's voice. I mean, did God *really* tell us, or was that just the way we wanted it, because hearing God's voice would make us better than anyone else? Abraham, I've been thinking. Maybe I've been too submissive all along. And if I have, I've betrayed myself. And us. Well, no more. You know why?

ABRAHAM: I'm not sure I can deal with this.

SARAH: Because I think God really doesn't want us to be submissive. I think God wants us to take a little responsibility for ourselves. Otherwise how will we ever discover if God is between us? We have to use the minds God gave us in the struggle to love each other and to live, and experience what it means to trust God. Don't you see, that's why we have to talk to each other. That's why there can't be any more hide-and-seek. We have to cock that third ear toward each other as well as toward God. Right?

ABRAHAM: Yes, I guess so. After all, something in me insisted on talking with you when I came back down the mountain. But I have to tell you, I'm still a little confused and frightened about it all. It's so different from everything I've thought and done. Maybe it's just too late for us, after all our betrayals and blindness, all the hurt.

SARAH: Abraham, listen. You said it yourself. We're still here. And so is Isaac, whose life I celebrate daily. And Ishmael, for whom I pray, wherever he is. As long as we're here, there are chances for us.

ABRAHAM: But what about all those betrayals? Maybe we've used up our chances. Maybe we're just too old now.

SARAH: All right, so maybe we have made a lot of mistakes, betrayed each other, and done a lot of damage. But something keeps breaking up the rock of our past so we don't have to keep dragging it behind us. Something keeps giving us chances to try something different. That's what's happening right now! Don't you see? Abraham, I think breaking things up is the point of God's story. Credit isn't the point. Or blame. *Chances* are. So what if it's taken us all this time and all these chances to learn. What matters now is *this* chance. God's in the future, Abraham, not just the past. Come on!

ABRAHAM: You don't think we're too old? You don't think it's too late for us? You really think we've got a future?

SARAH: Oh, Abraham. Sweet, stupid Abraham. I do love you, really. You have no idea how much more wondrous you are when you let yourself be just a human being instead of trying to be some kind of hero. Now listen, lover, third ear cocked: you're not so old that you can't remember, or figure out, that if we're part of God's story, our story's never over. And that makes everything possible. Makes it *promising*, even. Of course we've got a future. So, what's too old? Now listen up. You and me, we've got one Isaac. You know how we did that! Sure, it was mostly God's doing. But our part in it was pretty . . . well, exciting, wasn't it? And fun! How about we go find a place and try for another

one, do our part again? You're never too old.
Come on! What do you say?

ABRAHAM: Sarah, you break me up. You really do! Thank God.

(Genesis 16–17, 20–22;
Matthew 1:1–18, especially verses 1 and 2)

THE ODD COUPLE

I'm known as Jacob, which is a strange way to put it—strange but precise, because you may know my name but you don't know much about me.

To be honest (which is what I want desperately to be now, for all our sakes), I didn't know much about myself either until one night. One night it was, yet pieced together from a thousand days and nights which preceded it, each becoming a tiny cell, a quiver of a movement, a whispered layer unnoticed at the time, but accumulating slowly, surely, like buds on the trees, until one night I *did* notice. One night I could no longer avoid who I was. One night my life came together, or came apart, and I saw . . . no, more than seeing, I was *seen*, confronted. One night I collided with myself, yet with more than myself. It was a splendiferous collision. It left me with this ungainly limp, this holy brand in my flesh and bone, and this riveting walleye which is the permanent seal of my having seen something awesome.

Ah, those thousand accumulated days and nights. You spend your life doing what you have to do, or think you have to . . . not think, just *assume* you have to. But in the doing, things happen to you that you don't plan on, or think about, or want.

Occasionally, without warning, it seems a new thing happens or is just there—like a stubborn sapling pushed up inside the ruins of an empty fortress whose walls are scarred by vanity, stained by melancholy, echoing the loose rubble of shadowy intrigue and slobbered spoils. There the sapling stands, green and hopeful in a mottled shaft of sunlight floating down through an opening some stonecutter built high in the wall years before for no apparent reason except as a kind of personal signature that he'd worked there, a pebble of an impulse tossed in the pool of time to send out mysteriously beneficent ripples. And even though you live in those ruins, you don't really notice that sapling until one day you do see it, pay attention to it for the first time, though it's been growing there for how long? But I digress. Or perhaps I've just told you my story. No, not quite. It's not that simple.

As I said, you spend your life busily doing what you think you have to do; one thing, then the next, and the next, sometimes several at once. But, once done, there is never the time nor the chance to do them over. In fact it doesn't occur to you to look back, to do anything over, to change the pattern, because it's working for you. You are succeeding.

So you get ahead. Oh, it's never as far ahead as you'd like or think you should be, but you do get ahead. I certainly did. I did what I had to do, and it really had little to do with what people call morality. If the issue had been only morality, I wouldn't be disclosing myself like this. I am probing for something deeper.

Oh, there are always those who sit comfortably and self-righteously out of the arena, evaluating and criticizing according to their views and values—as if they had some divine right to do that. But, honestly, what do their values matter to you when you're split-lipped in the midst of the battle, the taste of blood and excitement in your mouth, victory in your sights? The truth is, their criticisms don't matter because the world isn't a snug and simple place, and critics are usually those who are untroubled by love or by complexities or by self-knowledge. They're people who lack the daring to try to create something.

All right, the record shows that I duped my father to get ahead. But it doesn't show that he was old, that all he seemed to care about was the state of his bowels, eating his fill of his favorite stew and dozing in the warm sun. Besides, before you rush to judge me, remember that my father loved my brother, Esau, more than he loved me. At least there was every indication that he did and, despite my efforts to compete with my brother, I failed in all the ways that seemed to matter to my father. So my love for my father turned to despair.

The truth is, the rivalry between my brother and me actually didn't matter because, according to our law, Esau, being the older one, would have gotten all the family benefits and privileges anyway. The system itself, sanctioned by our religion, was unjust, unfair. Wasn't that reason enough to resist and subvert it, by subterfuge if necessary?

Moreover, I had support in subverting the law. My mother, Rebecca, was tougher and shrewder than my father, and she loved me more than she did Esau. Or maybe she loved me more because Isaac loved Esau more, and we brothers were just caught in the undertow of my parents' clashing passions.

I can say that my mother's favor and manipulations made me a bit squeamish at times, as if, even as an adult, I was still just a mother's boy. Yet, mother and I formed an effective alliance and, besides, aren't you supposed to honor your mother? Does that requirement change if your mother is cunning and ambitious and has a plan to help you get ahead?

So, yes, I duped my father, and I cheated my brother out of what was rightfully his, according to the system. But, my brother was a bit of a sucker anyway—a hairy-armed, hairy-brained fool, to put it bluntly. So I ask you: Should the clear-eyed be held back by the slack-jawed? Should the quick be hampered by the slow? Should the world be penalized that way?

I didn't think so. Without a sideways glance and with a little deception, I managed to win; yes, win! First, I manipulated my brother out of his birthright. Then I won from my father, Isaac, the blessing he had intended to give to Esau. With the blessing came the advantages and inheritances of being first in the family succession. I hadn't committed a crime, just practiced cunning (I'd say *admirable* cunning). I'd manipulated myself into the favored position for gaining power and wealth.

And I got away with it. Of course, I made some enemies in the process. That can't be helped, can it? Of course, I envy and snipe at those above me, and those below me envy and snipe at me, but all that's nearly irrelevant. The essential point is, I got away with it and got ahead.

Oh, it's true that having gotten away *with* it, figuratively, I had to get away *from* it, literally. But isn't running what keeping busy is all about, all the rationalizing and excuse-making and blame-laying? Isn't running inevitably involved in succeeding? Of course! Oh, maybe when you've succeeded, you put on a modest face, do a little acting to protect your flanks and keep your essential intentions and operations covert. That's all part of running. In any case, one of the ways I ran was by leaving my home country. Esau was furious and threatened to kill me. So mother helped make arrangements, and I went to visit her brother, Laban, who lived in another country.

At the outset the running was a curious mixture of loneliness and exuberance. Then a strange thing happened. One night, shivering in my blanket under the stars with a rock as my pillow, I had a dream of a ladder stretching to heaven on which angels were going up and down. At the top of the ladder was a bright cloud from which a voice boomed forth promising to give me the land on which I slept, to make me rich. I just knew the voice was God's. It was a wonderful dream. It is wonderful to have your desires religiously confirmed. All those grand promises I'd heard Isaac ramble on about would come true for me. For *me*, not Esau. I was thrilled. Perhaps, reflecting on it now, I was a bit uneasy underneath for a moment. But it passed. The thrill prevailed.

But now I wonder if such a vision isn't really dangerous. It is always dangerous to believe that your way of doing things is right, your way of seeing things is right; that somehow you are better than someone else, that somehow you know the mind of God—though you might not admit it or put it just that way. But you'd *act* that way, wouldn't you, act as though somehow you had the right to decide who should be punished or rewarded, who is superior, who inferior—which sex, which race, which nationality, which religion. The terrible arrogance of believing you are right is dangerous, perhaps most keenly to yourself. Yet, that's what I did!

So, if you noticed an edge of that arrogance unsheathed in the views I expressed about Isaac and Esau a moment ago, you're right! But at that point, guilt, which is the underside of self-righteousness, hadn't begun to rumble in me yet. It was just a slight squeak of unease, of dis-ease that passed like a gas pain, and the rest was jubilation over the dream. I was confirmed in my course; I was destined to be a success.

So, I'd no more arrived at Laban's and fallen for Rachel, than I wheeled and dealed, and went hell bent for the bundle. I wouldn't have put it that way then, but now I would. The point is, success breeds repetition. What succeeds once, you do again, and again, never reflecting, never questioning. Block by block the fortress gets built. Yet slowly, almost unrecognizably, a longing begins to stir within for what is outside the fortress walls.

Still, what had worked with Isaac and Esau worked as well with Laban. We negotiated, made deals. Then we welshed, fudged, twisted loopholes around every provision. Whenever either of us got the short end, we'd claim to be injured, aggrieved, owed. It happened to me when I thought I had a deal to get Rachel for seven years of work, only to have Laban pawn Rachel's ugly, older sister Leah off on me instead. But since I really wanted Rachel, I negotiated another agreement: seven more years of labor for Rachel. But I sought a way to use those years to get even with Laban, to beat him out of his wealth. I found the way when I discovered how to breed the flocks to my advantage.

So for seven more years we agreed, cooperated, competed. And when it was over, I had won. And I felt right in winning. Whatever I had done underhandedly, in my view Laban had done more and worse. It's a relief when you can use the competition's methods to defeat him. The only thing that bothered me was Leah telling me I was just like her father. But I wasn't. I was a winner, he was a loser. That was a big difference. I came out of our deal with wives and wealth, sons, flocks, and servants. Laban ended up with depleted flocks and shrunken wealth because I learned a trick about breeding flocks, and I wasn't about to tell him about it. Thank God for the suckers of the world. I'd gotten away with it again.

Of course, Laban's sons weren't at all happy with what I'd done to take over their father's holdings, so I had to run again. But, as I said, running is all part of winning. What mattered was that

I had gotten away with it. Never believe anyone who tells you that you can't get away with something. The only question is how *far* you can get away with it.

I began to have trouble with that question as I high-tailed it out of Laban's country. I began to be nagged by the feeling that I hadn't gotten far enough away, maybe *couldn't* get far enough away with it. With Laban and his angry sons in hot pursuit, I found myself doing a strange thing. I don't know what made me do it, but somehow I found myself headed in the direction of home, back to Esau and whatever it was I'd been running from—though I couldn't have told you what it was or even that I was aware I had been running from anything, except Esau's wrath ripened by twenty years, and Laban's freshly cut and writhing wrath. I didn't weigh whose wrath was most dangerous. I wasn't caught between them. I could have run in another direction. My turn for home was instinctive, like the stonecutter leaving his hole in the fortress wall.

Yes, I had gotten away with it, but apparently not far enough. At night I couldn't sleep. I'd wake up sweating, the bed robes twisted, strangling me. I'd go outside the tent and peer into the darkness, trying to see something, anything that would explain my life, assure me. But there were only the silent hills and the silent stars, and the whispering wind—languages I didn't know. What troubled me wasn't so much the pangs of conscience as it was the cracks spreading like the webs of spiders across the inside walls of my fortress, as if weaving messages in another language I didn't know. And the mortar holding the walls together began to crumble, filling the air with dust motes, making it hard to breathe sometimes. No, what began to torment me wasn't conscience so much as the feeling of emptiness, the longing.

Sometimes, when the sun set below the far hills and turned the sky that soft, golden color which seems to come from somewhere far away—someplace you ache for but can't get to—and when the distant rills were shadowed in mist and a hawk circled it, sometimes then I'd feel my heart would break for the things I had not done, the unlived life that was haunting me.

Yet, you do what you have to do, or think you have to do! You take advantage of the opportunity to better your place in life, to build security for yourself and your family, whatever. But I began to wonder if I always knew what was better. Does anyone ever know?

Sometimes as we moved along, I'd watch the children play, or listen to a storm rage down the valley, or just look for a long time into Rachel's eyes. And then bits of questions would flash across my mind like falling stars across the summer sky—a sudden trail of light, quickly doused in darkness again. Sudden light, sudden questions: "What is it you HAVE to do, Jacob?" Then the sudden darkness, the groping. I'd squint into that darkness and listen to the hum of the servants' voices, the staccato of children shouting at their end-of-the-day games, the rustle of animals bedding down, and I'd ask myself, "What do I have to do?" Then the quick, familiar answer, "Why, provide for my family, of course."

But the answer was groping in the dark. I knew providing had become the exercise of transposing essentials into comfort, comfort into ease, ease into abundance. Success: you cheat for it, if only those you love; you steal for it, if only time, your life time; you lie for it, if only to yourself, about yourself. And, yes, you can get away with it, but maybe not far enough away. There are dust and echoes in the fortress, falling stars in the sky, the quick trail of light in the mind: "What is it you HAVE to do, Jacob?". . . and then the douse of darkness again. That's how my story unfolded, the story of a man you know by the name of Jacob but do not know as a man, unless you know me now.

It was as if some hook had been set in me, attached to some endless, invisible line, and wherever I went, something, someone at the other end gently but surely played me on it. I did things, and then without knowing quite why or how, I began to count up the spoils and the casualties. The casualties . . . the casualties. By referring to the casualties of my actions, I'm referring less to my guilt than to my longing, my terrible longing. Guilt was only part of it. The larger part was emptiness—all the things I had not done, and the time no one has to do any of it over. The blocks in the fortress started loosening and falling, little by little, because I had lost interest in keeping them in place. Or if not quite interest, then certainly I'd lost enthusiasm for the task. The sound of the falling blocks made echoes which stretched and stressed the emptiness of my fortress.

The casualties were my parents—Isaac, Rebecca. And my brother, Esau. And my wives—Leah and Rachel, both of whom I'd won and whose devotion I thought I'd earned. Now, standing by my tents at night, trying by the very intensity of my gaze to pierce the ocean of darkness around me, to glimpse the one who played the line on which I was hooked, I realized that Leah and Rachel were not so much victims of my arrogance as casualties of my betrayal of myself, misshapen by my unheeded longing, all the unlived things in my life.

I am not at all interested in turning my story into some tidy, edifying moral lesson with all the rough edges smoothed off. I detest such pious simplifications. I am not talking only about the state of my own spirit, as if that was all that mattered, or that it mattered most. No, what I am talking about is the connectedness of everyone—a profound, mysterious connectedness. All those thousand nights later I slowly began to realize my longing hinted at connectedness. It wasn't only me, my life, my future at stake in my struggles. We're all coupled, somehow. We're all at stake together, each with all, all with each. That is what I am trying to say about casualties.

We are the casualties of our own successes. We are always the casualties of our misdirected passions. There can be no easy designation of the betrayer and the betrayed, the offended and the offender, the perpetrator and the victim, the right one and the wrong one. We are always the casualties of our unlived lives and unheeded longings. Each of us. All of us. My family. My friends. Even my foes. Including God. Even including God.

In betraying me, I had betrayed them all. In betraying them, I had betrayed me. So that is how the days and nights unfolded. Of course I stayed busy. I was constantly on the move, as always. Only it was all vaguely different. Sometimes at night, or even in the middle of the day, an awful quietness would close in, fantasies of disaster would fill my mind, and sudden cold sweats would break out. Then I would have to get up and move, do something to muffle the sound, the cramp of the silence.

Or sometimes, watching the older servants, I heard the sounds of my own mortality in the shuffling and burping and squinting, and I'd sense it was more than my youth, more than my time I was losing. It was my *life* I was losing. It was the loss of life that lumped my throat in those golden sunsets, as I watched the circling hawk look for whatever she was looking for. Only it wasn't majestic hawks but drab sparrows that really plagued me. I had scattered the crumbs of my life behind me, and the sparrows of trivia had eaten them all, so I couldn't find my way. In the gathering dark their chirping mocked and tormented me.

At other times, even as I wheeled and dealed, even as I talked, I'd realize I was straining to make myself heard over the chatter of my own fretfulness, the twitter of my endless accounting and explaining, the cacophony of squadrons of sparrows. But there wasn't time to do things over. There was only the fortress, regal in appearance, a ruin in reality. And so we moved on toward the border of home, toward the River Jabbok.

Then one night it happened—something that out-grappled my words, a mystery with muscle, a shadow with the grip of a wrestler and the moves of the wind. What we think we know is only the small, manageable side of a larger, elusive underside. What we grasp is only a finger, a lock of hair, the movement of a lip, of even our own being, to say nothing of the body of being itself stretching away in all directions of space and time, past all space and time. We ache to know more. We pay people to tell us they know more. We want the mystery reduced, rendered manageable by a plan, an answer, a verifiable theory, a religious incantation, made into something we can purchase with a bit of coin, leverage with a bit of prayer or behavior or thought. We spend our lives trying to work that reduction and then, somehow, sometime, somewhere, at some Jabbok, we realize it isn't possible. The effort has been an illusion. Hard as it may be to live with unanswerable questions, it is not questions we die of, but answers: answers that get petrified into dogmas, swords, successes; answers wearing the ribbons of wars and wins.

So it was one night by the Jabbok, yes, but more than one night—a thousand nights of memory and regret, a thousand nights of restless longing shaped at last into an infant hope rocked in a scarred grandfather's heart. I cannot tell you very clearly what happened, except I wrestled, thrashing wildly amidst the whirling shadows and snapping twigs and shooting stars. I had sent the rest of my company on ahead, across the river. I was afraid of Esau, of course. Already I had sent messengers ahead with lavish gifts for him. But it wasn't Esau only I was afraid of. I was just *afraid*. Maybe just afraid of nothing. Yes, that's it, of nothing. It's fear like a hole in your stomach, fear of things around you fading further and further away, fear that your sweaty grip on things is slipping, slipping. I was afraid of nothing, of being swallowed up by it, getting lost in it, becoming it. I was afraid and alone. Alone, not just because the others had gone on, but alone in the way you are in those times when you realize that you are always alone in some inescapable way.

And I wrestled. With whom? A ghost? A demon? My self? Whom do any of us wrestle with when we wrestle with anything? I'll tell you what I believe with all my heart: I believe I wrestled with God. Don't press me on it, because when I first looked at the face of the one I wrestled with all night, it was the face of Esau. Then Isaac, then Rebecca, then Laban, then Leah and Rachel and all my children. Then a hundred strangers. And I had loved and wounded, and been loved and wounded, by all of them.

Finally, it was my face I saw in the adversary—my own face grimacing, weeping, screaming, straining against me, trying desperately to say something to me. But all I could hear was the panting of my breath, the sharp squeals and grunts of the battle, the river pounding storm-driven against the shore, the chirping of the choir of sparrows and, overhead, the cry of the hawk I'd seen circling in the sunset, a cry that resonated all the longing in my heart.

The memory of that moment is as fresh as the wind that rises now as I tell of it. As I wrestled, I began to hear something under all the other sounds—or deep within them. It was the whisper of that one I wrestled with asking, ''Do you love me, do you love me, do you love me?'' And answering at the same time, ''I love you, I love you, I love you!''

Then, finally, there was only the wheeze of my own exertion. And all around us a thousand stars seemed to be falling, splintering the blackness with bright slivers with that one relentless question: "What do you HAVE to do, Jacob?" I squinted to glimpse the questioner, but the slivers of falling starlight passed too quickly.

Yes, it could have been God. Really, could it have been anyone else? All I know is that it was an odd match, an odd couple. Still, it was a curiously familiar oddness, as if wrestling with God was something I'd been doing all my life, all unaware. And the strange thing was, that night I was winning, winning as I have always won. Winning with my tricks, my charm, my wit, my talent, my shrewdness.

And then suddenly I was crippled. Broken. Defeated. In a moment, curiously like the often sad moment immediately after sexual ecstasy, I knew I could never win what I really wanted, never achieve what I truly longed for.

In that moment, that tick of awareness, that cramp of desperation, I cried out. Pleaded, prayed out of all the need and longing and strange surging gratitude of me. "Bless me," I gasped. Before the words came, I had not realized it was a blessing I wanted—a blessing I could not name but could not live without.

"Bless me," I pleaded. "I cannot let go, will not let go until you bless me. Please." And deep inside I understood that the blessing I wanted, needed, had been seeking all my life was really not the blessing I had manipulated out of Isaac. Neither was it the sort of blessing I had tricked out of Laban: all the wealth, the wives, the sons. It was not a blessing I could win, gain, get with all my cunning and sharpness, with all my charm and guile. It was another kind of blessing altogether. It was something I could only receive, not gain; only accept, not win.

I think that blessing comes only when you are broken somehow—perhaps not visibly so other people know, but when you know that all your achievements are of little matter, when you sense you are empty. The fortress, however intact it seems, is in ruins and you realize it. And then, I cannot explain it, but then, somehow, there's the sapling, the little green tree reaching toward the soft, mottled light, that single shaft of light piercing the shadows. There in the ruins is that indomitable thrust of new life: the sapling and the unexplained opening in the fortress through which the light streams.

Stripped of all the trappings and poses of Jacob, I received that blessing. I became Israel. I became connected. I became a gift of the beginning of a people, of a family. To claim that blessing would take all the passion I had, all the chutzpah. Maybe God liked the chutzpah in me. After all, it was my sense of direction, not my aggressiveness, that was faulty. Saplings thrust toward the light!

So one night by the River Jabbok—on the border between yesterday and tomorrow, between where I'd been and where I was going, between what had been and what would be, between who I was known as and who I really am, between what was only possible and what began to actually be—I wrestled with God. And when for the moment the wrestling was done, I sat by the river in pain but at peace, drinking the air like it was water, drinking as someone would after a long trek in the desert, drinking air and the dawn as if they were life itself. Perhaps they were. I thought about what had happened, tried to make sense of it. When I had put as much together as I was able, one thing seemed clear. All those faces of the one I wrestled with had something in common: whatever their shape or color or texture, every face wore the expression of hope, as if looking for—and seeing—another chance. *Every* face, which surely included God's face.

Slowly I understood that, all my life, chances had come to me over and over again, but somehow I had missed the most important ones because I was afraid of the risk. It was easier to be Jacob the successful than Israel the faithful, easier to be Jacob the hustler than Israel the daring. I'd been afraid to be myself, to be Israel, the company of the new, the lover.

So I had a chance, not to do anything over but to do some things differently, which I think is what love is all about—holy chutzpah, daring to do it differently. That one night with a thousand antecedents began to have a thousand sequels. I was given the chance to face without flinching what I'd done and not done, and let it do me over. I was given the chance to begin to live the unlived life that haunted me. That's everyone's chance. That's what Israel's message is.

But it occurred to me that only when you sense, deeply, the connectedness of everything are you able to take that chance, to dare something different. Emptiness is emptiness, is nothing. The fortress is always in ruins, yet always the green sapling trembles in the light, as a chance trembles in every moment. The face of chance is the face of love. The face of chance is the face of God. That is my story, Jacob's and Israel's story, for I am both.

And my wrestling goes on. But it is a little different now: I am a bit friendlier with the foe and so with myself. But to be quite honest, my limp gets worse each day so I cannot run anymore. That, too, is strange blessing.

My last secret is that in Hebrew the name Jacob means "someone who supplants," someone who takes over, edges others out, gets ahead, is a go-getter. The truth is, there's a little of Jacob in me, in all of us, I think—maybe more than a little.

But Israel was the name given me that night by the holy stranger, and that name means "one who strives with God." There is a little—or a lot, really—of Israel in me, in us all. For striving with God is what we all do, finally, in all our striving. And to grasp that mystery is really the struggle of faith. It is the answer to the question, "What do you HAVE to do?"

But I've learned, through the years to my old age, that Israel means something else even more profound. It means "one whom God fights for." Now, with dim eyes, I see clearly that just as in everything we fight *with* God, so in everything God fights *for* us, with us and for us, even in the darkness.

And that is really our connection, our story. As both Jacob and Israel, we are those for whom God fights in all that goes on in our life, our connected life. That's what makes each of us an odd couple. A very odd couple. Awesomely odd. Every sneaky, tricky, cunning, self-seeking, flawed, forgiven, beloved, beautiful, connected one of us. So to you, by your Jabbok, I send my blessing, and pray you a limp and a walleye from God.

(Genesis 32:1—33:4;
Matthew 1:1-18, especially verse 2)

When the Calf Dances

Hmmm. . .the night slips away. . .slowly, slowly, darkness into gray, Sinai's mists softening into silver and rose. So it comes. Through the long stillness, I inhaled the shadows. Now I exhale the elusive secrets of the night, those wispy clouds of breath which scurry away into the cracks of light. Like a bewitched lover, I spent the night listening to the stars; floating through the sky with the moon; chanting strange incantations with the wind; watching, watching for signs and wonders, something clear, something solid as Moses' weighty slabs. Yet the night ends, but not my uncertainty. I cannot know for sure what the calf was about. I only know what I intended was something solid and certain as my brother's stones. Yet both the tablets and the calf lie broken now.

So the morning sun rises once again, reluctant yet proud as a youth from his beloved's bed. The wind begins to sigh gently, satisfied after the revelry of the night, gathering my presence into its embrace and settling down to rest and wait. It will be hot soon. In a little while we are to drink the potion my brother has made from the dust of the golden calf. Oh Moses, Moses, my brother!

Why does he insist on this ordeal, this trial? What will it prove? "Those on the Lord's side will suffer no ill effect," he says, "but the false, the corrupt will die." So, along with the others, I, Aaron, will take the cup from my brother's hand and drink it, and we will see which side I am on. But does anyone have eyes to clearly see

LIBRARY OF
FIRST UNITED METHODIST CHURCH
BURLINGTON, VERMONT

such things as sides? Are there, in truth, such things to see? If all corruption were to be seen, what else would we see? If all who falseness tainted were gathered on one side, would there be any on the other?

Ah, a little lizard. What makes you so bold? What do you want? Here...let me...aha, caught you! Maybe you won't be so bold, next time. Or will you? Easy, easy. I won't hurt you. There, there, let me look more closely at you. Such a curious creature. But then, aren't we all? Such a wondrous place this desert. All this rock and sand and scrubby bush. It's so harsh, so forbidding, so apparently hostile to life, yet so full of living creatures: spindly plants with delicate blossoms; tiny flowers that nuzzle the earth and set it afire; small creatures that scamper and wiggle and leap about—rabbits that look like gray rocks; rats that hop; lizards that change colors, letting their circumstances shape their identity, as if they shared my weakness and that of my people. Then there are lizards such as you, my fat little friend. How did you get so fat?

Easy, easy! I know you are afraid. I know there are wolves and owls and hawks about, and you must find your crevice before the sun gets much higher in the sky. Ah, but will you make it? That's always your question, isn't it? And I understand it better this morning than any time since Pharaoh's army was chasing us across the Sea of Reeds. I also know what fear is, little brother. I, too, have the impulse to scurry for a crevice, a place to hide. We have that much in common, little brother: fear...and perhaps our *handsome* countenance.

Yes, I joke. You are quite as ugly as I. Perhaps all attractiveness has been taken from us for a reason. I, to be made a priest of Yahweh not to be distracted by vanity from my duties. But what of the distraction of envy? Of longing? Are those distractions why I made the golden calf?

And you, why are you ugly? To help you survive in this hard place? No, surely not, for you are not less or more ugly than this place itself. Perhaps then your ugliness is to reveal the value of life in spite of appearances. If so, there is a kind of peace in that. Perhaps you are a sign of life and of peace in a hostile place. So I shall call you Ruach. Yes, that's it. Ruach—God's breath. Perhaps to name you that is the daring and the anquish of a man whose passions cause him to imagine too much...and to be lonely.

Ah, Ruach, I hold you captive in my hand and yet, would you believe, that I feel a shiver of fear of you? Surely, it is a dark and ancient feeling. Moses says your kind are unclean, and our kind are not to touch you or we'll become unclean, too. You see, even fearless Moses knows fear. I suppose all creatures do. It is, after all, a hard world, gnawed and chewed, frazzled, violent, even cruel. We feed each other and we feed upon each other. There is no guarantee of safety anywhere in it, my friend. No guarantee of much of anything except that we have to live and die.

We are vulnerable, so vulnerable. Still, we waste our days attempting to disguise our vulnerability, but when we deny it we are most dangerous, lashing out to defend what cannot be defended, groping about to wrap ourselves in the illusion of invulnerability. Probably that is also what the golden calf was about.

You see, little brother, my kind, my people were slaves in Egypt, and then we managed to escape into this wilderness. But we are certainly no safer here...just freer. Freedom has meant that we have to face just how vulnerable we are, and how we will come to terms with it and our fear of it. None of us does very well at that, do we? Here, Ruach, I will put you down. I will give you your freedom. Your vulnerability is more singular than mine, and your freedom less. You must find a place to hide. I only desire to but know I can't.

Oh, you aren't going to run away quickly? So! Maybe we are connected by more than fear, you and I. Yes, what surges beneath our fear is the same urge to live. It is life we share, is it not, the breath of life that is in us both. I named you well, Ruach. We are part of something larger and grander than either of us, aren't we? So we are in some way part of each other, I suppose. I do not understand that connection, my lizard brother, but just now I feel it deeply.

I do not have the words to carry the load of what I feel, any more than you do, your tongue darting in and out so nervously, mutely. But my kind are supposed to have the gift of words. I am supposed to speak with the tinkling flow of a stream in this desert, all music and clarity and brightness. I am Moses' tongue—his tongue, darting in and out at his command.

But, Ruach, silence is more eloquent. And more to be honored. Who can trust the one who can say anything? No one, not even the speaker. But Moses needs me. I am supposed to give wings to my stuttering brother's thoughts, his commands. Yet I cannot find the words even for my own thoughts, for the silences of my own heart. There's the ache. I try, I strain, I grope for words, but I cannot seem to find them. But I keep trying. Yes, I keep trying.

"The connections, Moses," I plead, "you have to see the connections. Please! Do not miss them. Do not deny them. All things are connected: creatures, the earth, the birds, the great fish, people, life is all connected. Where did all this—these living things—come from, if not the Lord, Moses? In the plagues those creatures—the frogs and the maggots, the flies and the locusts—weren't they all God's creatures? Weren't they God's doing? Yes! They must have been! There are connections among things, Moses, among us, all of us. Don't you see? You must not always be about separating, dividing, Moses."

But my brother, this giant of a man, shrugs and says, "I don't understand what you mean, Aaron."

And then I shrug and say, "I don't understand either. But that doesn't mean it isn't so. We must see those connections, my brother, we must acknowledge them. We must catch the rhythms and cycles of them, for they are *our* rhythms and cycles, the rhythms and cycles of life itself. If we do not affirm our connections, we will betray their Creator and reduce to triviality the mystery of creation. And if we trivialize creation, it will destroy us. Moses, before we control things, we must affirm the mystery of life—the same mystery we see in the way of the great river in Egypt running silent to the sea, then flooding mightily to bury, then raising the land to life. We must feel it in the ebb and the flow of the sea tides, the haunting play of light and shadow and color in this desert. We must acknowledge it in the way of a man and a woman fitting together, and then in the birth and children playing, and in a thousand ways, a thousand connections. Moses, a man becomes wise in seeing the connections and honoring them."

But, Ruach, about then Moses always interrupts and says, "We are not connected to the Egyptians who kept us in bondage, or to the creatures of the plague. You speak eloquently of false gods, abominations, diversions and idolatries. You echo the drivel of the fertility cults. Enough! Yahweh is a righteous God. Yahweh will have none of it. We are Yahweh's people, and we must obey His laws or He will put us away from Him. Obedience is required of us, and that is the whole of it. That is what we must do if we are to become a nation, defend ourselves, flourish. Let the offenders be cut off. We are *not* connected. Righteousness! Discipline! Obedience! Those are our watchwords."

"What of praise?" I ask. "What of praise, Moses?"

"Well, that, too," Moses answers, but always gruffly, as if his agreement alone constitutes the act of praise. Praise is quick, with Moses.

"But, Moses," I say, "praise does not issue only from clean lips, or pure hearts, if there be such. Praise is. . .praise is creaturely."

Ah, Ruach, I always falter just at that point. I don't know how to go on. Moses waves his hand in dismissal. And so our talks end. Often I long to tell him that, as far as I can see, righteous people seem to have only their own sense of righteousness to praise, and they greedily use the unrighteousness of others to glorify themselves. I want to tell Moses there is no virtue in that, only imagined achievement. But, instead, I just look at my brother with an ache and a deep admiration. Such an enormous man. He is right in so many ways. But, I believe, not in every way. We shall see. Shortly I will drink the potion, and we will see.

Ah, Ruach, you do not move. Are you listening, my tough-skinned little friend? So I pick you up again and hold you between my fingers. Shall I dash you against the rocks? It would be so easy! There is something in me that would gladly smash you, with savage urgency. Even to speak of it, to imagine it heals my blood in a surge of excitement. If I smashed you, as Moses smashed the calf, there might be a momentary feeling of triumph, a surge of power, of exultation perhaps, a sense of having eliminated some possible, fancied threat—as though by destroying you, I would be safer somehow. Oh yes, do not doubt the savagery in me, Ruach! I do not understand the sudden surge of it, almost like the heat of sexual desire or the growl of hunger which leads to the hunt. It is a frightening, primitive thing.

Yet there is something else in me, too, but no more understandable. Indeed, I am almost ashamed to mention it, for the weak thing I've been taught it is. Along with the savagery, is awe, wonder. You know nothing of that, do you, Ruach? I see how admirably you are made to live in this desert. I have seen others like you many times run to escape into a crack in a rock and then wedge in so tightly that no owl's claw or wolf's tooth could budge them. In the crack you lizards grow larger, more fierce. Ah, you are fearfully and wonderfully made, and I am fascinated and instructed by you. But can you see that I, too, am fearfully and wonderfully made; that I, too, am cause for awe? No! You know only fear, not awe. Can I myself see that I am wonderfully made? Yes, I can see that. I can deny neither my savagery nor my awe. Both are part of the mystery of me and of the way of things. But can I, who am awed, awe in turn, not just frighten? And whom should I awe? That, too, is part of the mystery and the uncertainty.

Quickly then, lest a savage impulse bid me otherwise, I set you free. You are still alive and still vulnerable, even as I am. So, rejoice! Or is that what you're doing when you puff yourself up to fill the crevice space against intrusion of the fang? Or is rejoicing a more human thing, the way my kind have of expanding to fill every corner of space with life? Or with golden calves?

"Praise," I say to my brother, "praise does not have to issue from clean lips..."

Then, alone in this desert at night I say, "Please, Yahweh, let it be that praise does not have to issue from clean lips or pure hearts. For I would praise you, and you know my uncleanness. Do not turn my praise back upon me, or I will stagnate. In the rottenness of it, of me, I will turn killer and killed."

But still you do not run, Ruach. Do you trust me so much? Here, crawl into my hand again. Ah, yes. But, why do you stay? Is it because you want to hear more? Or is it because you agree with what I say to Moses: "Praise does not have to issue from clean lips..."

Sometimes Moses will argue, "Perhaps not. But I know that lack of cleanness breeds corruption and defilement and death. We must have laws to protect the community, to govern our life, to insist on our being clean, or we will not survive in the desert or conquer the promised land. People must choose, Aaron." He says it with terrible ferocity, as if it is not the act of choosing itself but the options that torment him: "People must choose, Aaron."

I wonder why he is so afraid of his tenderness, his compassion, that he must keep it hidden, even from himself most of the time. Perhaps he fears it will kill him...and his people. Perhaps alone it would. But alone, his rage will kill him, too; and worse, make him a killer.

Still, Ruach, Moses is largely right. Vice is not the only path, but often it is the easiest one for us to choose, or the most attractive, at first. It is true, we do need guides, laws. We must be hard. Our savagery does need restraining. But often I get the feeling that it is not just restraining that Moses wants, but the elimination of the savagery, even though it mean the elimination of the savage as well. And there is the crack in his slabs of stone. For it is just at that point I think he misses the connectedness of things.

To be wise, one does not always choose between two things, but chooses to accept both. My brother rages at his own fear and fears his own rage, and then rejects both, turning them into "righteousness." So he misses the connectedness and the mystery of things. He sees sides...always. Two sides: right, wrong; good, bad. That's it. So he forces things. And in most things, in most circumstances, he prevails. Outwardly, he is intense, sure, strong, dominating. But inwardly he lacks the freedom of the larger truth, and so he lacks, as well, a sense of peace, a feeling of joy.

Perhaps you'll understand if I say that my brother is a lean man. He attacks. He is driven to reduce everything, shrink it into parts and then fit the parts together, just so, leaving out what doesn't fit. Yes, just so, *only* so. He traces steps to be followed to a solution, to an objective, to the promised land. So "here" becomes only a passage to "there," "now" only a strategy toward "then." He tells us we are to overcome obstacles, use things, control ourselves, achieve the goal.

Well, I am a plumper man than he. I say, "Wait, Moses. Maybe you can only catch life for a brief moment, like you catch a stream of cool water spurting from a goat skin bag. For a moment the thirst is quenched; for a moment, an incredible moment, the joy is experienced, expressed in a sigh or a chuckle that meets the water in the throat and becomes a fountain spouting pleasure to your nose, your skin, your belly, the hairs on your head; for a quick, glorious moment the back of your hand moves across your mouth to suck the wetness off, as with a passionate kiss of lovers. Then the moment's gone; but the joy was there, real, wondrous. That's how it is. Moses, look! Look at the flowers. Listen to the old woman who moves slowly and knows things. Enjoy the honeycomb. Take off your shoes, Moses. Bushes are burning everywhere."

But my brother smiles and plunges on like a spear hurling straight to the target. He begins to count on his fingers so he won't lose track. "One, two, three: God said, 'You shall have no other gods before me...you shall not make for yourself a graven image...you shall not take the name of the Lord your God in vain...you shall not kill.' "*

And I interrupt hopefully, saying, "Moses, what about the Egyptian you killed? What about the Amalek we slaughtered last week?"

Well apparently, for Moses, admitting to a little unrighteousness is like admitting to a little leprosy. With a wave of his hand he says, "That was necessary for us to do as God's people." And he goes right on..."Seven, eight, nine: 'You shall not commit adultery...you shall not steal.' "*

And I yell, "What about all the gold we stole from the Egyptians when we left?"

And he yells back, "Nonsense" and rushes on: " 'You shall not bear false witness...you shall not covet your neighbor's...' "*

"And that land of milk and honey," I scream at him, "do we not covet that with a vengeance?"

"God promised it to us!" he roars at me.

---

*Deuteronomy 5: 7–21, RSV

58

So I give up and find myself glad that Moses only has ten fingers.

Well, I don't mean that exactly. It's just that he is such a lean man. He counts, he writes lists; he wants to fasten things down, make sure of them, organize, draw sharp distinctions, get somewhere. Get somewhere!

So I gently suggest, "Moses, Moses, my brother, one cannot get from sunrise to noon on the word 'not.' A 'no' moves nothing. 'No's' *stop* things. 'You shall not. . .you shall not. . .you shall not. . .' If that's it, everything stops. 'No' is like a ten day fast, Moses. All right, fasts are needed, good. 'No's' prepare one for something. But for *what*? Think about that, my brother."

"Surely, there must be a 'yes' at the heart of it somewhere to move our hearts. Granted, your law is necessary. But, Moses, don't you see, the law can tell you how to bake bread, and when. Yet it cannot tell you, it cannot explain, how the bread is to taste in your mouth, how the sweetness of it feels on your tongue, what motions it starts in your soul, what music it stirs in your heart, what conversations it opens between friends at table. What about ecstasy, my brother? The law cannot start it. Only stop it."

Oh, Ruach, Moses simply doesn't understand what I'm trying to say. He only sees what his law and logic can do, which is much, so very much. But he cannot see what it misses, which is also much. So he simply shakes his head at me. I put my hand on his arm and I say, "And praise, my brother, what of praise?"

He looks so stern and he says, "To be righteous is to praise."

I nod and reply, "Yes! But could it not also be true that to praise is to be righteous?"

Ah, Ruach, then the thunderclouds gather over the sun of Moses' face and he storms away. My brother is a thin man and restless in the night. He paces and mutters. He does not like things to be shadowy and blurred. He ignores any hint of complexities or mystery. I think something in him wants to be invulnerable, to be so righteous that darkness and death will recede before him, not touch him. He does not see the connectedness of things, or trust it.

You, my little friend, you and I are more acquainted with the night and shadows, with the inevitabilities of life and death and love. So we risk dancing with them, don't we? We know the wonder of the way the wind sings, and the taste of salt on the lips, and the sudden sound of quail wings, and the sensuous caress of this desert. We know that life is cruel, as well as endlessly ingenious and wondrous, don't we? We can hear, and so we can wildly join the chorale of praise that floats up to the caverns of heaven from the snarling, burping, chirping, howling, squealing, rustling of this teeming life below. We welcome being nurtured by this earth, this mother who suckles us, in whose rhythms our very heart beats, and whose touch on our bare skin entices us to unspeakable dreams. We know.

Yes, Yahweh is on the mountain and, yet, Yahweh is also resident in these cracks and crevices, companion of us creatures here below, filling the space of us, and so, somehow filling the space of Himself. That's the mystery. So I say, ''Praise to that mysterious one we cannot name, or know, except beyond all knowing.'' To that One, I sing, I dance with you, Ruach. AHHHH...

Yes, little one, I made the golden calf, and now I will drink the potion Moses made of the dust into which he smashed it. We'll see who is on which side, if in truth the sides stay straight and do not braid.

I suggested to Moses that he exercise mercy, but he wouldn't hear of it. Yet surely it is mercy that keeps us, or Moses would never have been found in those bullrushes at the beginning, or escaped the consequences of murdering that Egyptian, or heard the voice in the crackle of the flaming bush. Justice by itself would be a cold light. It needs compassion to be a warm light, a burning bush. Without compassion we would not have escaped from Egypt. Without mercy, we would be in bondage always, forever.

So now mercy must keep us. Without mercy there is no hope for me, for anyone. Or is that only the plea of a weak man speaking in this last hour before the test? No, I think not. It is *fear* I fear, not death—fear made palpable in cruelty and stupidity, fear unleased in the shape of senseless violence, fear that wears the mask of arrogance, fear which snags the loose ends of questions and then tries to unravel the meaning of everything.

Am I a fool, Ruach, my lizard friend? Yes, of course. If I have learned anything, it is that I am a fool, however I try to appear otherwise. Sometimes that knowledge makes me more gentle than Moses with other fools. And sometimes it makes me more gentle with myself than Moses is with himself. I ache for this brother I love. But he does not allow for my love for him. His hardness will surely bring us to the promised land, but in doing so will also shrink the promise.

We are all fools. So before the sun rises much higher, we will drink the potion. But if I have come to believe anything, it is that someone, whose name we dare not speak, is not a fool, however it may appear to us at times.

Yes, I made the calf. The people wanted to worship, to celebrate. They were afraid, and their instinct was to turn their fear into worship. Their instinct was accurate, even if the shape I gave it was not, even if their interpretation of what I made was not. They wanted gods.

Yes! It is a deep, undeniable thing we all want. We want something to speak of the unspeakable, something visible to assure us of the invisible, something to contain a shimmer of the uncontainable. Is that not what our words struggle toward, and all our ache and fear and longing: the gods, The God?

The people wanted something that might hint at, that might connect. . .yes, connect. . .with life; with the mystery, the glory, the power, the love behind it all, through it all; something to hint at God! Is that not what we all want? Yes! Yes, it is, Ruach!

So I said, "Bring me your gold." And they did. Should I have made a *tree* with those rings and baubles they brought? A tree would have served as well, or a frog, or a fly, or a locust or a bird; anything, any of the creatures the Creator spins off so wildly in what must be exuberance, endless ingenuity, the ecstasy of creativity, Yahweh's ecstasy.

I took the gold and melted it, and made a lump, a shape, whatever it was, no matter. All right, it was a calf. But I swear, the shape wasn't at all what mattered. What mattered was that in the fire, on those rocks, the shape *danced*. The calf danced! I swear, the dance was what I saw. The dance is what I often see. The dance is what matters, not the calf—the dance! It is the whirl of creativity. Of God.

You, Ruach, my little lizard, I have seen your kind pursued so closely by your enemies that your life is in imminent danger and yet, at the end of your flight, you pause before you disappear into the crevice and, for the blink of an eye, you crouch and leap and whirl. You dance! You dance even while the talon is poised, the tooth bared. I have seen a thousand variations of that dance which even the spectre of death, nor all the ''no's'' ever uttered, cannot still. A thousand variations: in the light of a man's eyes turning toward home, in the fingers of a woman moving over the cheek of her child, in the play of an old man's smile almost lost in the landscape of his wrinkles until they, too, quiver.

Well, Ruach, I swear yesterday the calf danced, and I saw it. That's why I called the gathering a feast of the Lord. When the calf dances, when anything dances—whether out of anger or fear or grief or joy—the Lord is in it. That calf danced! And the sun danced, and the stars and the rain, and the whirlwinds of dust and of silence, and the flowers. . .everything danced. And my memories danced, oh yes, Ruach, my blessed memories danced: memories of green fields in an easier land, and my father planting in the spring, and my mother singing while she cooked supper as the evening light came through the window, following her about like a friend; memories of the taste of soup heavy with leeks; memories of many things, even things I never knew. Everything danced. Even the hair on my arms stood quivering, and my heart; every speckled, streaked, spotted thing danced. And I danced. And the people danced.

Ruach, it was glorious. . .glorious. But was it idolatry? I don't know, for idolatry, whatever it is, is not something outside yourself, something you can see or touch. What you can touch or see is an idol. But idolatry begins and ends in the heart, in the eyes of the heart, in what the heart makes of what it sees or does not see—maybe especially what it does *not* see. Idolatry is what the heart sees of God—or misses of God—when it looks out on the earth and its creatures. I saw the dance. And in the dance I saw the vitality, the ingenuity, the energy, the passion, the brashness of God. Ruach, there is nothing profane in what I saw, nothing unclean or unworthy in that vitality, that creativity. The holiness of that dance may be most of the holiness I will ever know, and it is a holiness you and I share: the creativity, the ecstasy of Yahweh. So I danced, that's all.

We are connected, Ruach, my little lizard brother, connected in our urge to *live*, not only to survive. For if survival were all, you would not pause to dance with the breath of the pursuer hot upon you. There are times when the calf dances, and I inhale the whole world in one breath, and in that moment I have breathed enough. I can breathe no more. I am full. I overflow. Beyond words I swell to some deep music. Then I feel nothing can get its claws or its fangs in me, and all I can do is dance, even without motion. My body, my eyes, my soul, the smell and sound and feel of me become a swoop of praise: a plunging, soaring act of love; a celebration of connectedness; an explosion of passion, of ecstasy. . . praise God, praise God, praise God. Praise God in the fang and the flower. Yes! I am a fool. Yes. . .thank God, yes!

I go now to drink the potion, Ruach. And we will see what we will see, little friend. But do you know what the deepest wonder of it all is? That it all matters so much to us! The mystery isn't only that we live and struggle and die. It's that we care so much about it all, so much that we devise a test and take it, and then, strangely, hopefully pass it. The whole of it is a mystery.

I wonder if you care, little friend. I think you do, in your lizard way. You don't understand my words, and yet you listen. Maybe it is my caring that you understand somehow. Maybe it is the caring of us all, all my brothers and sisters who will drink the potion with me and take Moses' test. We care so much that in all the struggle of our living and dying, we love and mourn each other. We scream and fight as if we hated each other—and we do sometimes. And sometimes we laugh together, and sometimes we spitefully reject each other, but underneath we know—at least some of us—that all the loving and hating and laughing finally speak of our being inviolably connected.

It is our caring, I suppose, that is so painful and maybe even harmful, and yet beautiful about us. We count things...and we wonder. We make laws...and we laugh. We seek righteousness...and we know we need mercy. We get angry...and we cry. We bash...and then we heal. We are proud...and then we bewail our pride. It's all connected in us. We're all connected: you and I and Moses, all of us!

And the connection, somehow, is the caring, even if we insist we don't care. All the time we really are caring—Moses, too, even for the Egyptians. I think that's why Moses balked at going back to lead us out. He knew it would mean bloodshed, and he cared, even then, for the Egyptians. They were his people, too. That's why he needed me to stand with him, to speak for him: to share the pain of the triumph. I was glad to be with him. I love him. Would that he would allow it. Would that I would. If we could only admit our caring to ourselves, to each other. If we could only see that the love, however faulty, is the ''yes'' in it all. If only Moses and I— and all of us—wouldn't make something deadly of our differences, something idolatrous. If we could just accept the differences as part of the connectedness. If only we could affirm the caring at our heart, at the heart of it all! For, yes, Ruach, I believe even you lizards care in your own way.

Oh Moses, Moses, the dance is really about the caring, the ''yes!'' The dance is because Someone isn't a fool, whatever the appearances may be. We dance in the palm of Yahweh's hand, even in this desert...even the Egyptians who dance in the shadow of death.

Well, little one. I put you down now. Be off quickly to your crevice. Remember your dance!

And I'll remember mine. I'll drink that potion. Will I live through it? No matter. Before I lift the cup, I will say to my brother, ''Moses, stay wide-eyed now, and I will, too. And we will see what we will see about sides and connectedness.'' I will look into his eyes, and I will say, ''I don't believe the dance will ever stop. 'No' is not the last word. 'Yes' is. Oh my beloved Moses, if only we could learn to dance together for the love of God. For the love of God, my brother, for the love of God. And for the love of one another.''

(Exodus 32)

UNDER COVER OF DARKNESS

If those jackals come back again, I swear they'll wish they hadn't! Mine won't be the only blood spilled next time. Torture me, will they? Have their stinking way with me, will they? Bastards! Damn dung heads! Just because I am a woman and they are the king's men, they think they can do anything they like! Well, next time they'll pay! Vipers! Camel asses! Hyenas! They actually howled in laughter all the time. Slobbering lust, twisting my arms, gouging, drawing blood from my soft places with the points of their knives, pulling my hair, holding my head back, their stinking breath gagging me, asking, "How does that feel, you dirty whore? Tell us where those men of Israel are or you'll get worse than this."

I kept thinking of those two men I'd hidden on my roof. "Don't move," I'd warned them, "don't even breathe. If the king's men find you, we'll all be food for vultures by morning and wish death had come sooner."

"The king's men," they call themselves. In a pig's eye they're men! They're animals, worse than animals, sniffing with their questions like jackals sniffing the wind for carcasses. So I told those bastards that the men of Israel had visited me, like other men, and for the same reasons, and then had gone their way before the gate of the city had closed. They roared at that and slapped each other on the shoulder.

"Did you hear that, boys? Even enemy spies visit the famous harlot of Jericho. So that's what they came for. Not a bad idea, huh?"

They winked, took their pleasure—all of them—and I let them, out of fear. Anything to be rid of them. I was afraid and outraged. But they said they'd be back to finish the job if they didn't find the spies. I'm sure they meant it. So now I listen for the shadows to rustle, wait for the crickets' song to cease, and keep a sharp eye on whatever moves by wind or breath or scurrying feet. They suspect I know more than I told them. Mangy, snarling dogs! I'll be ready next time. My knife is sharp.

Yes, the spies came to me. Sooner or later everyone comes to a harlot. They sneak through the shadows, trying to hide under cover of darkness so no one will see them, no one will know. They don't want to admit anything in the open, even to themselves. Oh yes, they come to me all right: the king's men and the king himself, soldiers, goatherds, merchants, thieves, priests, potters, silversmiths, wine peddlers, masons, well-diggers—all of them, they visit sooner or later.

Even their women come, sometimes in little groups to berate, to accuse, to assure themselves that they are not like me. I think they also come to deal with some terrible fear, to exorcise it, shed it and leave it here at my door where they think it belongs. But they seem always to come back again. They come to talk to me, perhaps because they know they cannot shock me, and I will understand and keep their secrets. Oh, some women only weep at first, but soon they also whisper some torment, some ache, some rage. They want me to listen to their stories, to answer some ugly questions.

So I listen, and I watch their eyes, eyes casting about in an urgent puzzlement and pain. Often I wonder what it is they want, why they somehow believe I—a harlot—can give them whatever it is. I listen, to some with my ears and heart, to others only with my body. Either way, the listening seems to be enough. They come and go, these men and women, under cover of darkness, and their errands have the feeling of life and death about them. But the next day in the market place they divert their eyes from me.

Ah, but we *do* want something from each other, true enough. The world turns on our wanting. We want something, always: olive oil, bread, weapons, wool, wine, a small trinket perhaps. Or gold, maybe, or power, or protection. Something. Some body. . .

somebody. The deeper the want, the deeper the darkness in which we seem to want to seek it. I deal in desires. Everybody does. Fortunes are built, kingdoms forged, reputations made—and unmade—in what we want from each other and how much we'll pay to get it.

Oh yes, we pay for what we want. There's a string attached to anything we get. We all see to that. We conspire in spinning the webs which entrap us. The more we want something, the stronger the string attached seems to be. My mother lives in the apartment downstairs. I keep her and my father there, pay all the bills. My mother speaks of love to me, and I hear "owe."

"I love you," she always says, "now be a good girl."

What could be clearer? I love...you owe. The curious thing is, I keep paying, almost willingly—fight, argue, complain, explain, but pay, always pay. I literally support her, and still she says, "Rahab, why do you do this to me? Such shame you bring to your poor mother!"

I answer, "Mother, why don't you move out if you are so ashamed?"

And she says, "Because I want to be near you, because I love you. It's for your sake I speak of these things. Oh, Rahab, you should give up this shameful profession. You should find a man, a decent man, Rahab, someone to take care of you, someone you can do things for. You should have children. You should be like other women. You should think of me. And your future. You should think of security and happiness..."

I listen and watch her eyes, and I see the familiar, urgent puzzlement. What is it she wants from me? She makes me angry, and I flare and point to my father dozing in the sun like a flea-infested old camel, his fondness for wine giving her an excuse to complain endlessly to the neighbors.

"Like you, mother? Happy and secure like you?" I scream.

Then she starts to cry, and so do I. Yet she provides my father with his wine. Perhaps his addiction is her security. And, yes, I provide her with the wherewithal to provide his wine. So pay...ah, yes, we pay. And we collect. Strings are on everything, and they get all snarled up.

Damn this pain in my belly. It's so familiar. It is morning's crying child conceived by night's crude coupling. They come under cover of darkness, and it is as if this body of mine held some secret that had to be kneaded out, clawed, squeezed, scratched, dug out for my night visitors' sakes...and for mine, too, I suppose, if all the secrets be told. Mother is right in a way: I do want security. I want at least some fragment of care, or what passes for it. So I've learned to submit. I've used what I had to get what I didn't have. Who doesn't? And what I had was my body. So I laid my self prostrate. Yea, I laid my life prostrate, hoping somehow the buried secret would emerge, be liberated by all that frantic groping in the darkness.

It is a weary business, a ceaseless round. Oh, I make money all right, more than enough. But the secret? No! That eludes me, as deeper joy eludes the orgasm. Each time, afterward, I light the candle and while the man counts the coins into my hand, I watch his eyes. Always I see the urgent, familiar puzzlement, as if the fleeting pleasure had somehow left the deeper wanting stripped and laid bare.

The men pay for different reasons, and in different amounts, but under it all I think each one pays in order to make what has happened an impersonal thing, to disguise his need, his mortality. They use their payment like a knife, something to cut away some part of time, some part of themselves and leave it behind. Then they won't have to deal with all of it, or all of themselves, or remember me, or even see me as a woman—not just a whore. Their money balances the account for them, makes it all only a brief transaction, a quick satisfaction—nothing else. But as they count the money into my hand, I see their puzzlement, and their pain.

Slowly, I've come to know that deeper wanting in myself, too. It is usually just before they leave that I feel closest to them, but I do not dare to mention it, or even feel it for long. They never look into my eyes afterward.

Last night the spies from Israel came. They had posed as traders and asked where services such as mine were available. Such requests are not unusual and raise no suspicions. The spies knew that a harlot sees things, hears things, picks up what is really going on behind the calculated appearances.

Darkness seems to encourage honesty, for some strange reason. What people hide from the light, they pour out in the darkness: their angers and their murderous impulses, their worries and fears, their dreams, their memories. Sometimes the men who visit me become almost like children in the dark, reviewing the day, examining their cuts and bruises and showing them with something like pride and hope; plotting tomorrow, wondering what it is all about; telling unbelievable stories that must be believed, somehow. . .and finally wanting to be held and rocked. But if I remind them of any of it later, they are quick to deny it, as if embarrassed. Or if I should say to them, "Yes, I know. I am like that, too," they just laugh and shake their heads incredulously and retort, "You? Ha! You are not at all like me." So instead of facing themselves, they manage to deal only with me; no, not me, with my body—my ears and sex. And they all come under the cover of darkness, as the spies from Israel came.

Those spies wanted information, and I gave it to them. It wasn't complicated or secretive at all. Not really. I simply told them that the people of Jericho were afraid, terribly afraid. And because of that fear, Jericho would probably be no match for the lean and hungry army of Israel. The spies came seeking information from me, and instead they got something much more valuable: they got courage. I don't think they realized that. Maybe they didn't want to. It may be all right for men to get information from a woman, but courage is another thing. Still, courage is what they got and, curiously, what I got from them as well. Strange how that works.

Why did I help them? I'm not sure. Once I might have taken them in because I am a woman, and women are supposed to make people feel at home, indeed make a home for them. But not this time. I was too angry at things. I wanted to put an end to my submission which I could see had become a way of dying in pieces. I helped them because I just wanted to *change* things for me. Yes, I think that is the truth of it. I'd heard this army was coming, and throwing in with them seemed a smart thing to consider because the people of Jericho had grown self-indulgent, complacent, and many of them were corrupt.

Or, to count out all the coins in my bag, maybe it was something about one of the spies, the one named Salmon. He looked into my eyes. It is an awesome thing to actually *look* into someone's eyes; the contact is almost frightening and nearly unbearably exciting. Maybe that was why I helped them. Or, surely, it was part of the reason. Yet there may have been a thousand reasons, but even taken all together, they could not explain why. But no matter. The truth is that I helped the Israelite spies because I helped them.

What I forgot is that frightened men can be the most brutal. Word passed quickly on the fear-polluted air of Jericho that the traders were really spies from Israel. Someone had picked up their accent in the wine shop when they'd stopped to ask where I might be found. So the king had been notified, and the king's men came searching in the night, their torches making the shadows dance grotesquely. When I saw them coming in the streets, I hurried the spies up to the roof by a secret passage sometimes used by customers. I hid them while the king's men pounded on the door with their sword butts. Then I hurried down to open the door. The king's men did not like being kept waiting.

I swear, if those jackals ever come again, I will cut their hearts out! But fear babbles bravely. And I was frightened, as frightened as the other citizens of Jericho.

When the king's men left, I got the spies and made a deal with them: my life for theirs. It took no special foresight to see there was going to be a battle here at Jericho, so I made them promise that if I helped them escape, they would spare my life, and my family's lives. . . *if* Israel could conquer this fortified city.

If! They laughed when I said that. They were so confident, then. A few minutes earlier, when the king's men had been smashing at the door, their sweat stank of fear and their bodies shivered as a young boy with his first woman.

"If," I said.

"No 'if'," they insisted. "Yahweh will give us the victory."

I told them I had heard of Yahweh. All of us in Jericho had heard stories of these curious people: how they had escaped from

Egypt and wandered around in the desert; the battles they had won, the lands they had already conquered. It was those stories that made the king and all his men tremble, and the rest of us as well.

We talked through the night, and the spies insisted it was Yahweh who won their victories for them. "Our God," they said, "is Lord in heaven above and on earth beneath." It was an enormous claim. Perhaps it is true.

"Yes, the Lord your God may be God in heaven above and on the earth beneath, but I saw you tremble when the king's men came. So if you escape, with my help, and if your army wins the battle of Jericho, you must spare my life. Swear to it."

They took a scarlet cord from a pouch and told me to tie it to my window as a sign so the army of Israel would know our agreement, and spare me and my family. As Salmon gave me the cord, he looked into my eyes. Suddenly the cord became like fire in my hand, a live coal burning through my flesh into my very soul. In that moment I knew the deal that I was plotting could not happen.

You see, I had thought that making this deal could keep me safe from both sides. If the army of Israel was triumphant, I would be safe because the spies would vouch for me. But if the army of Israel was defeated, I would still be safe, because the people of Jericho would not know about the spies or the deal I'd made with them, and the king's men could prove nothing. So I would survive either way.

But when I felt that cord in my hand, I knew such safety was not possible. If I tied this cord to my window, it would be seen. There would be questions. People would guess the truth. When they did, there would be no survival for me. The king's men would finish the job of killing me as they had threatened. And I gagged thinking of what they'd do *before* they killed me. Now *my* sweat stank of fear.

Still, if I did not tie the scarlet cord in the window, I would be making my payment to fear, cutting out something I had learned about myself in the darkness.

"If," I told the men from Israel, "*if* you escape and *if* your army wins. . ." They laughed again, and the laughter rolled easily, but I think as much from the courage I gave them as from the faith in Yahweh. Still, beneath the laughter they knew, as did I, that life always involves an "if." Life is always a choosing, a gamble. I chose. There, in that darkness that seems especially thick just before dawn and yet strangely fragile, I chose what seemed to me to be the coming of the light.

Then I lowered the spies over the city wall and told them where to hide, when to leave their hiding place, which way to go to confuse their pursuers. Will they make it back to their camp? Or will the king's men find them? I'll hear, soon enough. But will it matter, whichever way? That, no one can tell me.

Spies! Maybe I helped them because in my heart I'm a spy, too. Maybe we're all spies, in a way, spies trying to locate a promised land, a home we can settle into. That urgent puzzlement I've grown so familiar with must have something to do with our being spies looking for a homeland.

And yet, as soon as I felt that scarlet cord in my hand, I knew I was really homeless, that I would always be homeless. Not because I was caught between Jericho and Israel, but because, in truth, everyone is homeless. There is no place that abides. There are no walls that stand. Kings die. Battles are fought and won, or lost, and the winners and losers move on, one way or another. The old order is always being overthrown or collapsing of its own weight. What passes is only partly remembered, and what comes is only partly imagined. There is no abiding place.

Strangely enough, perhaps my profession is to make people aware of their homelessness. And yet I have seen that awareness in people's eyes, even as they come to me the first time. It is the *admission* of homelessness that is missing. If we could admit our homelessness to ourselves, admit that dark secret, maybe we would see that our only home is really in one another's heart. I think a home of some sort is what my customers are seeking when they come to me under cover of darkness. In a curious way it is also what I am seeking when I receive them. Only none of us knows it, or admits it. Maybe the darkness can still teach us the dark secret of our own hearts—our needy, harlot's hearts. I wonder if what we seek in the darkness isn't always but a breath, a touch, a tear, a laugh away, if we could only see and accept it. Yes, I think so. Maybe someday we spies will recognize the promised land, the promised chance, the promised time.

This cord. Dare I tie it in the window? Things change, but can I? I am afraid. Salmon looked into my eyes again just before I lowered him over the wall.

''I'll see you,'' he said. But will he? Will anyone see me? Will Salmon and his people even come back? And if they do, will they remember me, *me*—the color of my eyes, these wrinkles in my cheeks, the way my body moves, the tremor in my hand when I reached for the cord? Will they remember me—the harlot me, not some immaculate, virginal lie?

Will they remember themselves? Will they remember who they are, and where they have been, and where they are going under cover of darkness? Can there ever be that much of truth between us? Or mercy? Or love? We want something...and we pay. And maybe what we get for our wanting is precisely what we pay with: our lives. Maybe to get life, we have to risk paying with life—as a mother risks her life giving birth, as I risked my life with Salmon and the other spy. Is that what love is?

''If,'' I said to them. ''If...'' Now the ''if'' moves in the shadows around me and in me. Dare I risk tying this cord in my window?

It is dark tonight, starless. Yet, what I have discovered in the darkness is that life starts in the darkness: seeds in the earth, seeds in the womb, seeds in the heart.

''Yahweh,'' they said, ''is God in heaven above and on the earth beneath.'' Yes, but is Yahweh the God of the darkness as well? If not, I am left with only this knife, and that is darkness, indeed.

I will tie the cord in the window...and hope for a home in the heart of God. Yes!

- - - - - -

So it was that this story was told by Rahab to her son, Boaz, who told it to his children. And her story was repeated and remembered, until many generations later a father rocked the cradle of his infant son and recited the family history: ''Your genealogy, Jesus my son, goes like this. 'Abraham was the father of Isaac, and Isaac the father of Jacob, and Jacob the father of Judah and his brothers, and Judah the father of Perez and. . . Nahshon the father of Salmon, and Salmon the father of Boaz by Rahab, and Boaz the father of Obed by Ruth, and Obed the father of Jesse, and Jesse the father of David the king.' ''*

(Joshua 2, 6:22-25;
Matthew 1:1-18, especially verse 5)

Matthew 1: 2-6, RSV

WANNA BUY A USED CAMEL?

Hey, wanna buy a used camel? I can make you a very attractive deal here because we're trying to open up this market. *Very* attractive! Think about it. You could be among the first in your neighborhood to have one. Make you a trend setter. Get some free publicity, which wouldn't be bad for your business, you look at it that way. Plus, it'd be good for a few laughs, maybe. And, not to be overlooked here, very good for meeting members of the opposite sex. Who knows what all it might lead to? Think big, I always say.

Plus—now get this—think about the low maintenance on these beauties. No gas, no tires, no batteries; and it starts every time on cold mornings. And a little bonus: fertilizer for the yard, sell it to the neighbors for their yards. How can you miss? Like the camel said to the ox, "You gotta hump to be a camel."

Okay, it's a little slow for commuting—unless you go back and forth on that route you humorously call the "expressway." It would keep right up with that traffic. Besides, wouldn't hurt you to slow down a little, anyway. Might notice more things along the way. In the old country we had a saying: "The slower you drive, the further you go." Think about it.

If not for commuting, then how about for recreation? This baby'd be great for off the road action, take you where cars can't—backwoods fishing, camping, stuff like that. Plus, kids would love it for birthday parties, bar mitzvahs, Halloween, Christmas pageants, things like that. It'd be dynamite. And how about this: you'd have the raw material for camel hair coats at five or six hundred per each. Think about it.

And get this: we've developed this product called Camel Scope. (You may have heard about camels having bad breath.) Well, you mix these little pills with the water your camel sucks in every three or four weeks and, presto, the bad breath is history. Year's supply free with every purchase.

Now you may be thinking that you don't like the idea of it's being a *used* camel, because you don't get warranties with a used camel. Well, that's true, but tell me—do you get warranties with babies? Or with husbands or wives? Or with jobs? Or religion, or education, for that matter? Is there anything that *matters* that comes with a warranty? Think about it!

Let me tell you something. We're all used, everyone of us— you, me, even the little kids around here. You really think there's anything *un*used in this world? I mean, how do you think any of us got here if we didn't get a little used on the way? Everything's already a little used when it pops out of the womb, or out of the ground, or out of a mold, or out of your mind, or wherever things pop out of. *Used* is what we're dealing with here! Everything's frayed, bent, dented, scarred, a little worn at the edges, thin at the center. I mean, *everything*. Let's face it, "used" is the name of this business. It's called "Used Life, Inc." So let's not kid around. The question we're dealing with here is, "How do you handle 'used'? How do you do business on those terms?"

So you're thinking, "There's a little con in this pitch." Maybe there is! Also you're thinking I'm not the kind of guy you'd buy a used camel from. Again, maybe. (I won't bother to ask what kind of guy you *would* buy a used camel from!) I'll just confess that, yeah, I am more than a little used myself. In fact, I'm what you call dead— which I admit, is slightly more used than you are. But think about it! For the very reason of my being dead, I may have a couple of interesting points to pass on to you, so don't move on to the next used camel lot quite yet—no pun intended.

Let me try to give you the big picture here. First off, I lived a long time ago when things weren't quite so certain as they are now. Or maybe I should say people weren't so certain about things as they are now. We were a little more open to a variety of . . . possibilities, shall we say. What possibilities? I'm getting around to that.

See, there was this nasty famine where I lived, which was near Bethlehem, in the country of Judah. I mean, it was a *nasty* famine. Just wouldn't quit. So, being pretty shrewd, my old man—Elimelech was his name—didn't wait around for disaster to wipe us out. He took me and my brother, Chilion, and our Ma, Naomi, to this other country called Moab because there was food there. That move alone qualified him as a good father, as far as I'm concerned. Hungry kids make a bad father, is how I'd put it, so starving kids would make a lousy father, right? Anyway, I was grateful to him, partly because of the food, partly because Moab was where I began to learn something about ''used.'' By the way, my name is Mahlon—not nearly so cool a name as my brother, Chilion, got, but you can't win 'em all, right?

To get on with it, after we'd been in Moab a while, my old man died. We weren't too good at diseases back then, so I don't know what did it: the water, maybe, or the worry, or a piece of bad lamb. Whatever it was, the result was the same as it is now. First he got real hot, then he got real cold, and then the breath left him. So long, end of Elimelech, right? Not exactly. Just a little more used, you could say. Real hot, real cold, real used is how it goes.

The thing is, because of my old man being shrewd, there we were—me, Ma and Chilion still breathing, all right, but breathing Moab air which was a little complicated. My old man might have been dead, but he certainly wasn't gone either, any more than I am now. He was still connected, if you see what I mean. Think about that as we go along here.

So, like I said, when my old man died, me and Ma and my brother were on pretty shaky ground there in Moab, being foreigners with no status, no money, no connections. Talk about warranties! That's when I'd have wished for one if I'd known there were such things. Since you wondered about a warranty for a used camel, I'm sure you can imagine how powerless we felt when my old man gave out on us, stranding us in Moab. When you feel powerless, you want warranties, guarantees. Thing is, in used things—like life—there aren't any.

Well, that's when my Ma took over. Let me tell you, my Ma, Naomi, was one tough lady. No nonsense given, no nonsense taken! With Ma you knew where you stood, and where you stood usually felt pretty good. With my old man scarcely in the ground, my Ma said, "Boys, time for you to pick out a woman and get married." What she really meant was that it was time for us to get a job and support ourselves. Ma knew that having wives would keep me and Chilion out of trouble and hard at work instead of playing around and expecting someone else to pick up the check. Getting married is a pretty responsible step to take. You gotta have a job to pay the bills for the family, right? Think about it. Obviously, Ma had.

So I managed to hook on as an apprentice to a shrewd camel trader, whom I tried to interest in Ma—figuring it wouldn't hurt anything for her to marry us into a fairly well-off family, only she claimed he smelled bad and wouldn't have anything to do with him. I couldn't argue about him smelling bad, and it dawned on me that he'd been hanging out with those camels for too long. So I figured I better get a move on and find a woman before I started to stink too bad myself.

Anyway, I checked out the local eligibles, and Ruth, a real beauty, was the obvious one for me to go after. My brother, Chilion, who'd apprenticed to a candle maker, went chasing after Ruth's friend Orpah, which worked out well because we could double date on one camel. Anyway, I guess their families felt sorry for us, losing our old man and being foreigners and all, because they agreed the women could marry us, and the women didn't resist much, so we did the old "for better or for worse" bit. Little did we know. I mean, *little* did we know.

Because, like everything else, marriages and families are like used camels: there are no warranties. To begin with, Ruth and I couldn't have any children—or at least we didn't have any. I might have blamed Ruth except my brother and his wife didn't have any children either, so I decided not to raise a fuss. It might well have ended up splattering all over Chilion and me, since chances are it was probably something on our side of things that was at fault. Now, you gotta remember that not having children was a very big thing in those days. It meant not having anyone to take care of you in your old age, which gave some folks the idea that God was punishing my brother and me for something. I can tell you that was a heavy load.

But not having children as old age insurance turned out not to be much of a problem, because neither my brother nor I lived to be old men—which shows you how misspent most worry usually is. My brother spilled a vat of hot candle wax on his legs, and the burn never healed. His legs turned black, and the blackness crept up his body until, God forgive me, he began to look like a black candle, with his pale face and suddenly white hair as a wick. Honestly, I used to wonder what would happen if you lit him. No pun intended, but those are wicked thoughts to have when visiting a sick brother. Anyway, my brother turned very hot, then very cold, then very used, in relatively short succession.

Shortly after that, I was test-driving a used camel one day and, instead of paying close attention, I started thinking about my brother and how much I missed him. The camel must have sensed my preoccupation because he lurched and threw me off. My head hit a rock, and I skipped the very hot phase of the process and just went from very cold to very used immediately. My last thought—or maybe actually my first thought—was, "If you don't pay attention, it's amazing how fast you can go from being a little used to being very used." Think about it.

When I talk about "used," don't think I'm talking mainly about death. No, death's just an extreme example to help you get the point. Actually, "used" is mainly about life. And don't get restless; I'm seriously getting to the point now.

The thing is, the religion I lived by, the Jewish religion, has rules to cover almost everything that could possibly happen in human affairs. Those rules go back to when Moses got them from God up there on Sinai during the Jews' exodus from Egypt. Now I thought a lot about all those laws and why God gave them to us, and I finally decided God gave us all those laws about everything because God didn't want us to be bothering Him all the time about every little thing.

I mean, think about it. God's got a lot on His mind, running a creation as big as this one. We knew it was pretty big, even back then. We couldn't begin to count the stars we could see with our naked eye—though we didn't know it was "naked" then. After all, what's a "naked" eye? What's an eye *supposed* to wear: microscopes, telescopes, mascara? Anyway, naked eye and all, we knew the universe was enormous, and besides, when you consider all the wars and killing and cheating and exploiting and lying and complaining that go on in this world, and multiply it by all those other stars and galaxies and planets, you know God's got other things to do than to jump every time some branch manager or dissatisfied customer whistles in this world. I mean, God never came running when I whistled, so I figured the law was it. Got a problem? Look up the solution in the book of regs, right? Kind of a cosmic IRS, Better Business Bureau, Licenses and Inspections, Marriage and Family Counseling Agency all in one.

So God gave us these rules. Not warranties, mind you, but repair instructions, so to speak. To keep something from going wrong, do this; if it goes wrong anyway, do that. By giving us those laws, God could get on with other business, check His other franchises, so to speak.

Anyway, there is a long section in Jewish law dealing with the "used" condition. The part particularly relevant to this story has to do with what happens to women when their husbands die. The brother of the husband must marry the widow and provide for her. And if there are no brothers to take up the slack when one brother dies, then it's the next closest male kin, and so forth and so on, till you find some available male member of the family. That one has to marry the widow and provide for her. Since you can't be careful who your brother actually is, nor check out his longevity chart, at least you gotta be careful who your brother *marries*—check her out, advise him on her desirability. Frankly, women should be just as careful to check out their intended's *brothers*, for that matter.

Now, there's no arguing that those rules take the notion of family seriously—dead seriously, you might say. You could even say the family was something of a used sister-in-law lot, or a used brother-in-law lot, or a used cousin or nephew or uncle lot, and so on, ad nauseam.

However, the point is that since both my brother and I were out of the picture, and since there were only two of us to begin with, my wife, Ruth, and Chilion's wife, Orpah, were stranded. Talk about used! Well, even though I was supposedly out of the picture, I made a deal with certain "influential parties" which enabled me to hang around behind the scenes to see if there would be any small thing I could do to help Ruth out—nothing obvious or enormous, maybe just pull a little string here or there. You see, I felt bad that my klutsy brother had hot waxed himself to death so he couldn't be around to help Ruth out, and, to tell the truth, my brother felt ticked that I ended up with rocks in my head so I couldn't help *his* wife out.

So what happened was this. My Ma, gutsy old Naomi, sucked it up and decided to go back home to Judah—to Bethlehem, to be exact—partly because things had gotten better there by that time, and partly to relieve her daughters-in-law from having to worry about her. She figured if she left them, they could crank up a fresh start in their old neighborhood where they might cash in a few of the I.O.U.s they'd gathered over the years and maybe work out something to get them another husband. The way Ma looked at it was that she wasn't about to start having babies right then, since her best offer was the camel dealer she couldn't stand the smell of, and even if she did, she couldn't produce a husband for either of them for twenty years or so. Anyone who can count knows that would be a little late for Ruth and Orpah, all things considered. I mean, think about it!

So there I was, feeling a bit awkward lurking around, listening to Ma explain everything to Orpah and Ruth. Being invisible and inaudible was new to me, and I hadn't quite gotten the hang of it yet. As I worked at it, I began thinking the odds were ridiculously high against Orpah and Ruth getting another husband anywhere, since they were really used, having been married to my brother and me for ten years or so. Well, I wasn't surprised that Orpah took Ma up on her suggestion to stay in Moab. Orpah must have been figuring the odds the same way I was and decided her chances might be better in Moab. So she told Ma she'd stick around the old neighborhood.

But not my Ruth. Ruth threw back her shoulders and said to Ma, "Where you go, I will go, and where you lodge, I will lodge; your people shall be my people, and your God, my God; where you die, I will die, and there will I be buried. May the Lord do so to me...if even death parts me from you."* Now when she said that about not even death parting her from Ma, or from God, I got this funny feeling that maybe Ruth understood that death was just an advanced case of used, and somehow she could see me hanging around there. I quick ducked behind a tree. (I know I didn't have to do that, but I told you I hadn't gotten the hang of being dead yet.)

Anyway, crouching there behind the tree, I started reflecting on things. First thing was how much passion Ruth had. I always knew that, but this was a little different from the passion she'd shared with me during our marriage. I mean, now she seemed to be linking up passion with doing something against the odds. Somehow she seemed to know that passion was about nine-tenths persistence, persistence in the face of great odds, that passion was seeing things through, especially "used" things—since they're the only kind there is. Now think about that!

Another thing Ruth seemed to know was that passion involved an even bigger understanding of family than those rules and laws about "used" I told you about. I realized with sort of a shock that if she was right—as I felt fairly sure she was—then the family thing goes way past just blood relatives, which is big enough, but also goes on to "your people shall be my people."

Now, if you go that far, it means we're all responsible for each other, however used we are, just like brothers-in-law are responsible for their widow sisters-in-law. That's a big notion. I mean, Ruth was talking about family that cuts across national boundaries, and racial and religious boundaries, even cuts across the boundaries of death so that none of that separates us from each other, like it or not. And right then I wasn't so sure I did like it, because I knew some really rotten used camel dealers I'd just as soon have nothing to do with. But family is family, so we better learn to like it, 'cause that's how it is with us used creatures. Right?

Ruth 1:16-17, RSV

But the most startling thing Ruth seemed to be saying was that passion involved God. I mean, Ruth got God mixed up right in the middle of everything. Not just God's *rules*, but God—the very One than which there is no whicher, if you get what I'm driving at. What I'm saying is that if God isn't off somewhere checking His other franchises, so to speak, then where is He? How is He involved with our transactions, as it were? Think about it. I did. Those were the questions that got me right in my ethereals, you might say, and started me wondering. From that point on, I hung around to learn and to work a few things out.

Briefly, here's how the story came out. When Naomi and Ruth got back to Bethlehem, me wagging along behind them, Ruth went out to glean behind the barley harvesters—you know, pick up whatever bit of grain they had missed—so she and Naomi might have something to eat. It turned out the field she chose to glean in belonged to this guy Boaz who was one of the wealthier dudes in the greater Bethlehem area. Whoever said, ''Genius is nothing but an enormous capacity to choose,'' got that right. Because Ruth not only chose the field of wealthy old Boaz, but Boaz was also a decent guy, and, best of all, turned out to be a long lost cousin, or something, of my dead but not gone, only quite used, father, if you are still following me here.

Well, it didn't take Boaz long to fall for Ruth, and she for him. I blush to tell you that put me in a twit of jealously, even in my very used state, which is what I meant by saying I hung around to work a few things out. Anyway, after a time of dickering and conniving on all sides (which warmed my used camel dealer's heart), Ruth and Boaz took each other ''for better or for worse''— and both of them had been around the block enough times to not demand any warranties from the other. Sooner or later, you got to learn to trust, right?

The thing is, I had to ask myself why I kept hanging around even after I saw that Ruth was doing okay, after she first met Boaz and I knew it would come out just fine. Then I realized I was hanging around not so much because Ruth needed me, but because I needed her. I needed to learn something from her, or with her, before I could move on to another country, so to speak, as she had done. What I needed to learn was that there is "used," and then there is "*used*," if you know what I mean!

See, what I mean is everyone is "used" just by existing, like I already said. But beyond that, some people, like Ruth, choose to be "used" in a different way. I don't mean they choose to be exploited, or to be door mats, or malignantly nice, or sticky sweet "yes" sayers and "no" livers or any of that phony stuff. I mean they choose to be "used" by taking risks. They "use" themselves, so to speak. Or you could say they allow themselves to be "used" by some power in them or beyond them, you know, be open to new possibilities, be different, be creative. It's the kind of "used" that has something to do with love, I think. Think about it!

Well, I hung around a little longer for the wedding because it felt good to do that. Actually, I hung around the wedding wine jugs, sneaking a swig now and again for old times' sake. I even shed a tear because I was honestly happy, and I kept whispering as loud as I could, hoping someone would hear, "Our wildest fears exceed even our wildest hopes, but more often than not, our hopes prevail if we pursue them with passion, which is to say, with guts and persistence." That's a pretty hefty thought for a used camel salesman, don't you think? I don't know if anyone actually heard me, though once in a while someone would stop what they were doing, brush away something from their cheek as if a spider thread had just touched it, and look very thoughtful.

That encouraged me, so I also kept whispering, "There are often two fools in every transaction, and both for the same reasons: each asks too much of the other, too little of himself." I still don't know if anyone heard me. It doesn't matter. They'll learn. You'll learn. Besides, who listens to an invisible, tipsy, used camel salesman, or a camel used salesman, or whatever, at a wedding? Or anywhere else, for that matter?

Now, just a couple more details so you'll get the whole picture as I see it. I totally stopped being jealous of Boaz when I realized I'd learned more of the truth about "used" than he had. I mean, not just about blood family being responsible for one another, but the idea of family as terrifyingly, wonderfully bigger than blood relatives because we're all in it. I mean, all of us. People say, "Blood is thicker than water,'' right? But the fact is, "spirit is thicker than blood,'' and it's spirit that connects us all up, or in, if you know what I mean. What I mean is that what you call kingdom is really just "Used Life, Inc.'—which is another word for human family, though there's "used'' and then there's "*used*,'' don't forget. You follow me?

Okay, another important detail: even though Ruth was in her so-called old age, she conceived with Boaz. I suspect it was her passion did it. They named the kid Obed. And Obed was the father of Jesse, who was the father of David. Right there in Bethlehem. Right there where, a few generations later, the one you call Jesus was born, who was of the same genealogy as David, and thus of Obed, and Ruth, and indirectly, even me. Okay, okay. . .to include myself in that is a bit strained, but the point is, you just never can draw boundaries around family to know very clearly where they start or leave off. Think about it. The more, the merrier, as the saying goes.

The final detail is that I've started wondering if maybe God might not be a used God, too, just as we are used creatures. I have a hunch that God shares our dents and frayed edges and scars and that may be a clue as to where God is, how God is involved in our transactions. I mean, it makes some sort of crazy sense that God just might be hanging around in the used neighbor, the used kid, the used parent, the used brother or sister, or in-law, or out-law, doesn't it? I think that's what happened to me with Ruth. But if I can find out more, I'll let you know. Or someone will.

In any case, remember, there's "used'' because you exist, and then there's "used'' because you choose. And I'll tell you, I think the secret of the kingdom is in the "used'' because you choose.

So, wanna buy a used camel?

Okay then, how about a used camel salesman? As a trial offer? Might help show you how to be a good used self! What do you say?

Deal? Deal?

I certainly hope so. I need the commission.

(Ruth 1-4;
Matthew 1:1-18, especially verse 5)

THE CLOWN

If you had been looking, that long ago day, you would have seen a group of boys sitting in an uneven semi-circle around an old man sunning himself on a bench jutting from the wall around Jerusalem. Everyone was laughing in pitch with the old man's cackle. The boys were slapping each other on the shoulders, as nine and ten year olds do. The old man was Obed, my grandfather. Actually my great-grandfather on my father's side, though I always referred to him as my grandfather. I was one of those boys sitting at his feet that day. My name is Ithream.

I adored my grandfather. To me, there was no one like him. I loved to be with him, to walk with him, listen to his stories, ask him questions. Just sitting in the sun with him gave me a feeling of being part of something that would last forever. I was a middle son of many sons, and he understood the struggles of that for he, too, was a middle son and knew what it was to be overlooked in the family. No one paid much attention to my grandfather. He had spent his life building his flocks for his son Jesse who had inherited the wealth and became famous as the father of my father, David, the King. So I swore that someday I would tell the story of my grandfather so he would not always be overlooked. And maybe the best way to tell his story is to recite just what happened that one afternoon, for in some way, that afternoon gathers it all up.

So there we were, my friends and I, laughing at the feet of Obed because he made people laugh. I think many people thought my grandfather was stupid, a buffoon, but they didn't know him. He was wise, and it was in his wisdom that he made people laugh. And yet, sometimes I would find myself feeling a little embarrassed for my grandfather, and protective of him, because many of his teeth were missing and he tended to drool a little on his chin and the front of his robe. So sometimes, in my desire not to have my friends think badly of Obed, or of me, I would speak a bit harshly to him, trying to prompt him. If I hurt him when I did that, he never let on.

If you'd been listening, that long ago day, you'd have heard me say to him, "Oh, grandfather, don't say things like that. You know that isn't true. Stay with the truth." It was my awkward effort to apologize to my friends for the old man.

"Ithream," said the old man, shaking his finger in mock rebuke, "I am not your grandfather. I am the father of your grandfather Jesse, who was the father of your father, David, the King. I may be a very old man, but you seem to be the one who's confused." The laughter broke out again.

In spite of myself, I laughed, too. I so loved this old man. "But still, father of the father of my father," I argued, "is it not the law of Yahweh that even old, old, old men should tell the truth?" Obed put his head back against the wall and laughed louder than any of my delighted friends at my retort. I was proud because he was pleased with my humor.

"But, you see, Ithream," Obed finally sputtered, "finally, laughter *is* the truth. At least, it is a way to the truth, a true way. If people can't laugh—laugh at themselves and the strange things that happen—then they stray from the truth. They begin to take themselves too seriously and think of themselves as better, or perhaps worse, than they really are. That's why, when he was about your age, I taught your father, David, to play the harp and dance."

"Oh, Obed, tell us that story again. Please, please!" The request came from several of my friends at once. Obed knew which story they meant. He'd told it to them many times.

Slowly he got to his feet. "Those were happy days," he began. "My son Jesse and his sons and daughters had such good times together. We sang and told stories and laughed with one another. I would do funny tricks for them. I would tell stories and do little dances, and they would laugh and call me Grandfather Clown. Obed the Clown. Yes, those. . .were. . .happy days!''

His voice trailed off, and his eyes squinted as if peering through the mists of memory to another time. Then, as if transported to that earlier time, he poised himself unsteadily and began to do a little shuffle of a dance, his arms lifted rather feebly toward the heavens. But his youthful spirit overextended his physical capacity, and he lost his balance. He fell back on the bench. ''I love laughter,'' he concluded with a gasp, almost to himself. ''It is like a prayer.''

''The priests wouldn't agree,'' one of my friends ventured.

Obed smiled, as if jolted back to the present. ''No,'' he concurred, ''they wouldn't. They say prayers as if they'd just eaten a green persimmon.''

That image made us laugh, for the priests, whose breath often smelled slightly sour, always seemed upset by the idea that any of us should ever have a good time, so they were forever making our lessons in the Torah harder and longer.

Obed laughed with us and then, still laughing, said, ''Never mind the priests. The Lord may agree that laughter is a prayer. It keeps you in balance. Maybe that's why the priests don't laugh. They always seem to be tilting to one side or the other, weighed down with some heavy burden.'' He stood and mimicked the priests' stiff-legged walk, and we laughed again just as he toppled once more onto his bench.

Gasping a bit, he went on. ''Boys, it's hard to pretend to be something you are not when you're laughing—especially at yourself. Besides, laughing is a way of being penitent. The priests get so pompous and solemn about being penitent, insisting that we buy pigeons or lambs from them to offer as sacrifices for our sins. It's never *their* sins, is it? So they make other people pay for those sacrifices, and the result is everyone gets afraid of Yahweh's demands, His punishments. It's hard to believe the priests mean it when they speak of forgiveness. At least, it's hard to believe they think Yahweh forgives anyone. Does anyone think anything can change? No! Everyone begins to look like they ate green persimmons themselves. To have a chance to change things, change yourself, you have to believe in forgiveness: Yahweh's forgiveness is like sweet wine, like dancing and music. That's why laughter's a better way of being penitent. I think laughter is the true sacrifice of a contrite heart. We aren't God. We aren't animals. Balance is the thing. You boys agree with that, don't you?''

Before we could respond, Obed had closed his eyes. Still, we all shook our heads vigorously in agreement, not understanding much of what he said but simply agreeing because he had said it, and instinctively liking the part about sweet wine and music because we could relate to that. But quickly we became afraid Obed would doze off, as he did so easily these days. My friends nudged me. ''Tell him to go on,'' they whispered.

''The story, Obed, the story,'' I pleaded with him.

Obed opened his eyes. ''Oh, yes.'' He got to his feet again, steadied himself with one hand against the wall. ''The story. Those were happy days,'' he began.

''You told us that part,'' I reminded him, not too gently, afraid my friends would get bored.

''I did?'' Obed replied. ''Oh, of course, I did. So where was I?''

''The part about my father,'' I answered sharply.

''Oh, yes. David. Well, let's see. Of all Jesse's children, David seemed to understand best about singing and dancing and laughing. Even as a boy, he wrote little songs, something like the poems he writes sometimes now. I think he understood his grandfather, the clown. He understood about both the perversity of people and the goodness of life. And he understood that it's also the other way around sometimes: people being good—or trying to be—and life being perverse. Anyway, he understood how perversity and goodness are often at war in us and around us, causing us despair, like fishing in a lake with no fish in it. Ever do that, boys?''

Of course we all had, and so we fell all over each other telling about our experiences, and how stupid and angry they made us feel. When Obed figured we'd gotten the point, he went on.

''So you know how it is sometimes. Well, so did David, better than most. But he also understood that laughter is a gift from God, a balm, because it gives a kind of healing, a truce, a season of peace, a chance to change things. In knowing that, he was rare. He understood that laughter is like a bridge over which people can walk to themselves and to each other. You see, boys, people can't be enemies if they can laugh together. And you can't hate yourself much if you can laugh at yourself. The thing is, nobody taught us how to laugh. We're just made that way. It's the Lord's doing. Laughter is the material of bridges. If you don't laugh, you break the bridge to your own heart, and to other people's hearts and to God's heart.''

My grandfather had begun to wax a bit eloquent and was getting carried away. And my friends were getting restless at the old man's wanderings.

''The story, Obed. Get back to the story, please!'' I spoke more sharply this time, wanting to keep my grandfather—my great-grandfather—from losing the thread of the story, and his audience. Embarrassment was edging up on me.

''Oh, yes, the story,'' Obed said with a sudden start which made him lose his balance. He put out his hand against the wall and steadied himself again. ''The story. Those were happy days,'' he began again.

''No, Obed,'' I interrupted, with a grimace toward my friends that combined criticism of my grandfather with a plea for their indulgence. Their eyes were fixed on Obed. That flustered me and provoked me to an even harsher tone. ''Can't you *ever* remember, grandfather? Begin with my father being king.''

Obed laughed and bowed, whether in obeisance to me or to an imagined presence of royalty it didn't matter because it was obviously a mocking gesture. He spoke solemnly, in matching mockery. ''The king, Ithream? Oh, yes, the king. We must not ramble before the king, must we? Forgive me, your majesty. Oh, yes, King David learned well the ways and reasons of Obed the Clown. After many battles, and after he became king, David moved the palace from Gileah to here, Jerusalem, which is now known as David's city. You all know that, of course.''

We nodded solemnly, taking our cue from Obed, glad to be part of the drama.

Obed nodded back and continued. ''Of course. So you also know that to move the palace and the seat of government, David had to move the Ark of the Lord. And, of course, you learned men know that the Ark of the Lord is the most sacred thing in all Israel.''

We all nodded again, murmuring agreement, trying to control our giggling and feeling flattered to be called men, let alone learned.

Obed went on, shifting rather quickly from solemnity to gaiety. ''Well, as that sacred box which symbolizes the presence of Yahweh, the one and only true and eternal King, as the Ark came into the city, David stripped off his royal robes and began to dance and laugh and sing before the Ark as it was carried through the streets. It was a most happy occasion.'' Obed gathered his robes in his hands and tried to whirl about on his thin, hairless legs.

I leaped up and caught Obed just as he began to fall again, and helped him sit. Breathless now, propped against the wall, he was still muttering, ''Most happy occasion. Most happy. Dance. Yes, he danced and danced and danced.''

As if on signal, and to vent their pent up energy, my friends jumped up and began a wild dance together, pounding each other on the back and singing at the top of their lungs, though it sounded more like shouting: ''Praise the Lord. . .praise Him for His mighty deeds. . .His mighty deeds. . .His mighty deeds. . .His mighty deeds. . .''

It takes no imagination to see that we were particularly impressed with mighty deeds, as young boys are, and shortly the phrase took on an hypnotic quality. But no matter what had started us, shortly we were swept up in a kind of wild frenzy which spoke both of our exuberant years and of a timeless, primitive rhythm of sheer exaltation which seems to resonate most freely in youngsters and fools. The exercise was obviously a familiar one for us; we had done it many times before.

''Yes, yes,'' Obed laughed as we danced, ''that's the way it was.'' He clapped his thin, dry hands in cadence to our leaping, twirling song. After a few moments, we fell exhausted to the ground, laughing, rolling on our backs, feeling gloriously spent. Finally, we sat up.

''Yes,'' Obed observed, beaming at us, ''that is how it was. It was good—a happy occasion, most happy. You see, by dancing, King David was honoring God, demonstrating with his clownish behavior—which I had taught him—that there really is only one King: Yahweh. By his foolishness, David revealed God's wisdom. Yes, remember that, boys. One day you will understand. It was a good, glad thing David did. It was like setting people free. They joined with him in the dance, in the singing and the laughing. The sound of it rolled down the streets and out through the gates and echoed across the hills. It was a great moment, like the day of creation itself, when Yahweh said it was all good and must have laughed Himself. Oh, you should have been there. But. . .'' Obed suddenly stopped laughing and squinted again through the mists of memory.

"But what?'' we asked in chorus, leaning forward to hear the end of the story we already knew, but knowing, too, in some deep way we couldn't have put into words, that the end of the story wasn't really the end at all because the story was about us, and our children and our children's children.

"But what?'' we insisted again.

"But some people didn't like what David did,'' Obed replied soberly. "His wife, for one. I don't mean your mother, Eglah, Ithream. I mean Michal, King Saul's daughter, the one David married to try to bring harmony to the kingdom and peace to Saul. Michal didn't like what David had done. She had been royalty so long she believed it. But many others didn't like what David had done, either, it turned out. Do you know why?''

Of course we did because we had heard the story before. But in a deeper sense, we did not know because it made no sense to us. So we shook our heads, and all of us said, "No. Why?''

Obed looked at us, and I saw the sadness in his eyes. "No,'' he agreed, "you don't know why. Well, those people said a king shouldn't behave like a clown. It was beneath his dignity. And it dishonored God. They didn't understand. They just didn't understand that taking things too seriously—like being a king, or anything else—makes you afraid, and fear makes you turn sour after a time, and sourness turns to sadness, and sadness turns to sin. Of course, people are fools. That's what the story of Adam and Eve is about. But Yahweh is no fool. Anyway, fools should laugh at themselves unless they want to be damned fools. There isn't any laughter in hell. In fact, I think lack of laughter *makes* hell. But some people, the persimmon eaters, didn't understand any of that! Trouble was, they seemed to persuade David of it. He started taking himself too seriously. I think that's when all his trouble began. But that day, when everybody laughed and danced, was a great day, maybe the greatest day Israel ever had."

Obed was suddenly aware of how quiet we had gotten. The warm sun, our frenzied exercise and our difficulty following the latest part of Obed's story had made our eyes droop. This time, Obed realized on his own that he had to retrieve our attention. He lunged unsteadily to his feet again and began his old man's shuffle. "Praise the Lord..." he wheezed, arms outstretched, and magically we were revived and watchful, breaking into smiles. Activity we understood. But once again, after a short whirl, I had to come to Obed's aid. I caught him just in time—though I suspect he planned it that way—and helped him to his seat. We waited for him to catch his breath.

Then I asked, "But, Obed, why do we have kings if they aren't supposed to be...you know...kings?"

Obed winked and shrugged. "That's the riddle, isn't it, my learned friends? It's a big riddle, too. An enormous riddle." His eyes, twinkling, swept the group. "Help me with it. Do you think we need a king?"

We looked at one another a moment. It always seemed like a ridiculous question to us. And, as always, we nodded and, one after another, said, "Of course we need a king."

Obed pursed his lips and nodded sagely. "Yes, you're right, we do. Kings are useful. They are powerful. They give off an aura of order and security. And they are exciting and attractive. There's always a lot going on wherever the king goes. And it is true that, one way or another, we need leaders to help us organize and govern ourselves, and move toward our dreams. Sometimes kings do that well, but maybe not as well as shepherds tend sheep and farmers grow olives."

We didn't know what Obed was talking about. This was another part of the story that always puzzled us. We were all thinking of the glory and adventure of being a king. It seemed wonderful to us.

So when Obed asked, "Well, which one of you would like to be king?" without hesitation every one of us yelled, "Me! Me! I would." And then every time, after our outburst, we'd look at each other sheepishly, aware that somehow we'd exposed again some secret, some private desire that made us vulnerable in our ambition and greed. Then we laughed, realizing we all had the same desires and didn't really need to hide from each other. In fact, because of our mutual exposure we could be easier, closer than before, if we could just follow our laughter to the truth of us. Sometimes after the laughter, we'd touch each other on the shoulder, or rub each other's hair, like it was okay between us.

"Yes," Obed confirmed again, chuckling, "of course you would all like to be king. Everyone would like to be king or queen, I suppose. But you see, my friends, as long as you can laugh at that desire in yourselves, you keep it in balance. It's a foolish, natural thing about us—wanting to be king, some secretly, some not so secretly. It's part of the riddle—everyone wanting to *have* a king, on the one hand, and everyone wanting to *be* a king, on the other. Ah, which is it? Either way, or both, there is danger, isn't there? But laughter helps us keep it all in balance, you see. Of course, you see because you are such bright young men."

Again, in a blush of pride, we punched each other's arms and giggled for a moment or two. Then I asked the next question. "But you said we needed a king, didn't you, grandfather?"

"Yes," Obed agreed, "I did. You were listening, weren't you? Just for that, some sweets." He reached into a fold in his robe and threw a bag of sweetmeats to me. "Be sure to share them," he instructed me.

As the bag went around, I asked, "But, Obed, if we need a king, what's wrong with *being* a king?"

"Now that is the main part of the riddle, isn't it?" Obed nodded. "There's nothing wrong with being a king, any more than anything's wrong with being a shepherd or a farmer or an engineer, or a priest or an olive merchant or anything else. We need all of them, and we all need to be one of them. The riddle has to do with figuring out power and, therefore, with knowing what a king is and what a king is not."

"How did we get kings in the first place?" asked Joab, one of the youngest of my friends, knowing that question came next.

But his question always provoked the same reaction from the rest of us. We ridiculed him. "Everyone knows that. You are dumber than a jackass, Joab."

Obed laughed. "We all are, Joab. Hee-haw." On cue, we all started hee-hawing until we sounded like a herd of jackasses, getting down on all fours and kicking at each other and laughing because we got the point.

Obed finally interrupted us when he thought we'd released enough restless energy for another session of talking. He began to answer Joab's question. "We got kings because people wanted a king, thought they needed a king, just like you boys do. I remember it well. Samuel was a prophet who seemed to have a peculiarly close relationship to Yahweh. Yahweh spoke to Samuel, Samuel told us, and we trusted Samuel. He was our leader when we were just a band of separate tribes settling the land around here as far as you can see. Look around and see how far the land stretches."

Dutifully, we obeyed. It was a beautiful land, falling sharply away on all sides.

Obed stood to show us what happened. "I kept my flocks on my land way over that way," he pointed off to the south. "One day, not far from my land, people came looking for Samuel. I saw them and followed along. At last they came to Samuel, twittering like birds before a rain. 'Appoint a king to govern us,' they clamored. I started to laugh. It seemed a silly thing to ask for. So I decided to show them how silly I thought it was. Like the clown I am, I got down on the ground and crawled around on all fours like a crazy little baby, making crying sounds. They didn't get it. They thought I was crazy and pushed me out of the way. The message of clowns is often missed. But not by Samuel, which is why he was to be trusted. He laughed. He knew what Obed the Clown was saying."

"What *were* you saying, grandfather?" I asked dutifully.

"I was saying that life is hard, sometimes, full of difficulties and struggles. So, like a baby, we want a king to take care of us, to make everything come out all right, to love us like mothers love their babies and try to fulfill all their babies' wishes.''

We all made faces and expressed contempt. ''*Eeeuuu*, babies. Who wants to be babies?''

Obed clapped his hands. ''That's just it. No one and everyone. But that doesn't matter, really. Because no human king can make everything come out all right, anyway. No human king can fulfill the dream we have to be taken care of. Samuel tried to tell them that, too, but they insisted on having a king anyway. I have a hunch the people really knew no human king could do all that, but maybe they were being sly, clever as foxes. Maybe, like spoiled children, they really wanted a king, so they could blame him for their problems if he didn't solve them, if he didn't do the impossible and make everything come out right.''

''So what happened?'' asked Benjamin, my fat friend who was usually teased unmercifully by all the rest of us for looking like a roly-poly baby.

Obed beamed at Benjamin and said, ''You have a great and admirable hunger for knowledge, my friend.'' Benjamin buried his head in his chest, but his smile lit up his whole face.

Obed went on. ''Well, Samuel decided the people could have a king but, rather than appointing him, Samuel made them choose their king by drawing lots. So I started laughing again. Only this time, I grabbed a cloak from the richest man in the crowd and started parading around, putting on airs and pushing people around.'' To demonstrate, Obed got to his feet and puffed out his chest, took a few strutting steps, and pushed a couple of us over before sitting down again himself. We laughed at the charade.

''But why did you push anyone?'' I asked.

''I was showing them what you learned-friends already know and just demonstrated to each other. Everyone wants to be king. Everyone wants to make things go the way they want them to, make other people do what they want them to. Only most people can't laugh about it as you did. So they lose their balance. Laughter helps people keep from falling because of their dizzying pride and hunger for power.

Now, as you know, my friends, everyone has power of some kind. We can speak. We can act. We can learn. We can teach. All that is power. The problem is how you *use* your power. And for what. If you don't laugh at yourself to keep in balance, sooner or later you will use your power in ways that hurt other people. Most people deny their desire to be king. They pretend to be unselfish and humble and all that. They deny what's underneath. They deny their power, or their hunger for power, and their denial eats at them and then they eat at others. Everyone eats but no one's hunger is satisfied. But you, my friends, are powerful already and will be more powerful as you get older. And you do not deny it.''

Once more we were flattered and felt taller, stronger, wiser because of Obed. And, of course, we wondered who the people were who denied their power, even though we had a vague idea about the one he was talking about. But when we had finished our preening and our pushing and razzing, we looked again at Obed who had sat down. We thought for sure he had dozed off this time. My friends looked at me and insisted, loudly, ''Ask him, Ithream.''

Without opening his eyes, Obed smiled and said, ''Ask me what, Ithream?''

We all laughed nervously, then gladly as Obed joined in. He was a wonderful, amazing old man.

So I replied, ''*Who* denied their power, Obed? And what happened to them?''

Obed got to his feet once more, heaved a great, weary sigh, and said, ''I thought you were not paying attention and would never ask. Now that you have, I am glad to answer. In a curious way, Saul denied his power when he got to be king. He forgot that being king meant being *different* from shepherds and fishermen, not better. That's when he became a tyrant. He took himself too seriously and misused his power. He couldn't laugh at himself or help the people laugh. Now, David struggles with the same temptation. He must remember to laugh. Maybe kings have more power than most people, but it's just a human power. It's good to be able to build things, like this city David has built. But our power can destroy things, too, when we forget its limits. Our power *is* limited, you know! That's what laughter says: our power is limited. David knew that once. Maybe he will remember it again. There's only one power that's unlimited: Yahweh's. So we can laugh as free people...free...people."

Obed's voice had grown weaker with all his talking. He put his head back and lifted his face to the warm sun. We were all pensive now, drawing idly in the dust, scooping it up and letting it run through our fingers, amazed that it felt so much like silk, so much like Obed's words felt as they ran through us leaving a film of understanding which made us open ourselves to him so his words could run through us again, and again.

Finally, almost absently, I asked, "Will there ever be a good king?"

Without changing position, Obed spoke, his voice seeming to come from a long way off. "I didn't say David wasn't a good king."

Surprised at his answer, I insisted, "You know what I mean, grandfather."

"A Messiah, you mean?" The word sounded strange on Obed's lips. "Yahweh's king? I don't know. But we have hope."

"Will such a one rule...like my father?" I asked.

Obed opened his eyes and squinted into the distant sky, this time as if peering not into the past but into the future. "Like David?" he mused. "David is such a human person. I love him. I love him and I ache for him. He is a lonely, honest man, and faithful in his core. A Messiah like David? Perhaps, in some way. But maybe with a different kind of power. Or maybe not so different, just a power He will trust more and so will not lose, as David may have lost his. I think it will be something like the power of laughter, of some kind of unshakable joy. Probably people will think such a One strange, a clown of sorts, not like a king at all. Somehow, I think He will enable people to laugh, to not be afraid, to be glad in Yahweh. I always thought when I helped people laugh, it was a way of loving them. I'm sorry they didn't understand that, didn't laugh more. It might have helped them be a bit more free, like some of them were the day David danced and laughed before the Ark. And if people don't hear and join in the laughter, they will miss the King Yahweh sends... Oh, that was a day, such a good day, when the laughter echoed out across those hills. It must have rolled clear to the stars. It was such a day! Listen, listen, boys!"

Obed shut his eyes and put his head against the warm stone wall. As we grew quiet, we became keenly aware of the noise in the streets about us: shepherds moving herds to the market place, bells tinkling; children playing; women talking to vendors; the pleading of beggars; all the sounds of the streets in David's royal city.

Then in the midst of the babble came the sound of someone laughing, faintly at first, as deep in the throat the bubble of it built and rolled, rising as a sensuous tickle to relax the mouth, easing open the clamped teeth, the tight lips, enabling the sound of it to pour out like wondrous music, like the liberating trumpet of Gabriel, like the reassuring flute of the shepherd in the night. In a flash of frightening yet wondrous revelation, we realized the laughter was coming from Obed, Obed the Clown, the father of Jesse, the grandfather of David, my great-grandfather.

Obed's laughter leaped, as the breath of God must have leaped into Adam the first day of creation, leaped the generations to me, so that I began laughing from some deep, distant place within, yet a place linked to the farthest unseen star in the farthest unseen heaven. As if with a life of its own, the laughter danced from Obed and me to my friends, then splashed from us across the alleys and streets of David's city as it had once, long ago, and might once again. We laughed with the old story we loved and knew and yet had still to learn.

As he laughed, Obed nodded his head joyously and sang in the croaking sound of his aged voice, "Ah yes, come, come you kings, come. 'Praise the Lord...Let everything that breathes praise the Lord!' "*

And so our laughter built, rising to the highest point of the city, and rolling out and down over the valleys below, adding a curious glow to the golden light of the sun as it washed over the land.

Thus, as he had lived, did my grandfather, Obed the Clown, die that day and go to sleep with his fathers, as my people say.

---

*Psalm 150:6, RSV

But to say that he died is not quite right. What he did was pass on his life, and his laughter, to us, to me, as he had to David. And so it passes on, and on. To end his life in laughter, as a clown, was Yahweh's gift to this wonderful old man. And for me to be with him when he died like that was a blessing, though I miss him very much. Yet, some days, and nights, I still hear his laughter. It comes as a mercy and a joy.

And if you, too, listen very deeply beneath these words, beneath the noise of the street, beneath the silence under the silence, you will hear that laughter as well. It will sound like a prayer, like dancing stars, like an angel's song, like a beating heart, like the love of God. Happy will be the day we kings become clowns, for not to laugh together may be to miss the One who comes as a Clown to tickle us to life.

(Ruth 4:13-17;
I Chronicles 2, 11, 26;
II Chronicles 23;
Matthew 1:1-18, especially verse 5;
Luke 3:32)

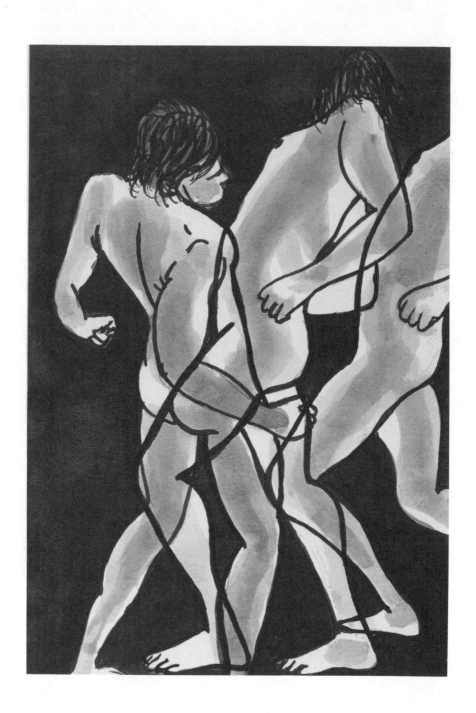

A NAKED TRUTH

Is there any one who cannot easily think of things he wishes he hadn't done in his life? No, from king to beggar, we all remember such things, often with great pain. But now, long after, I see that the secret of life is in discerning what it is you really wish you *hadn't* done, before it is too late to do something different. Perhaps the one thing I, King David, can give you is my story as a clue to that secret.

In the spring of my life, when sandalwood and promise scented the air, I danced. There are those who say the young dance because of the promise and the sandalwood. Actually, it is because of the dancing that one catches those sweet scents, for then, as now, there were also the sour smells of danger and stinkweed around. You see, dancing moves where words can't go and carries what thought is too leaky to bear, and I inhaled the promise.

So I danced, even after I was annointed king. Then one day—it seems like yesterday—I stopped. My wife, Michal, ridiculed me for dancing, and I never danced again. She saw me dancing in public before the Ark of God and criticized me for wildly whirling around half-naked like that.

"You don't know how to be the king," she yelled. "You are shameless, crude, vulgar. You are a fool."

Oh, I protested. I argued. But underneath, I believed her. Oh God, I believed her. I asked her, "What is there about you that wants to believe the *worst* about me?"

Michal snorted, "Because it's the truth."

I felt a spasm of fear. What is there about us that believes others are right when they believe the worst about us? I believed Michal, and I stopped dancing. That is what I wish I *hadn't* done!

The day I danced, though, I couldn't help myself. My heart was full. The Ark is the symbol of God's presence, and I was dancing before God. Yes, even more, I felt I was dancing *with* God somehow. I danced without thinking, without evaluating the reasons; I danced with passion, abandon, exuberance. It was a spiritual thing.

Have you ever seen lambs leap in the field, suddenly, without warning? Have you seen puppies chase their tails, kittens spontaneously jump and whirl, and colts prance and shake their heads? Have you seen babies pull themselves to their feet, and laugh and bounce to some secret music? Do they dance because it feels good? Do they move to the ingrained rhythm of their mother's heart beat? Or is it to the rhythm of the stars and moon? Or perhaps is it to the hum of God?

Surely, the answer is, "Yes, yes, yes," and that was the way I danced, and why I danced, that day before the Ark of God. Curiously, I recall my feeling as one of trust. Perhaps you've known that feeling as well: that primitive kind of confidence that enables you to leap and whirl, and know the earth will catch you, and something under the earth will catch it. As best I can tell it, my feeling was abandonment, trust. It was as though, that spring, I knew I would smell the sandalwood even in winter.

Then came Michal's words, her ridicule: "You fool! Control yourself!"

I was embarrassed. I believed her. I never danced again. That was the day I became king.

Do you recall the day you became the king or the queen? Perhaps it was less obvious for you than for me. But when *was* the last time you danced, or smelled the promise, or leaped in a crazy entrechat, and knew the earth would catch you, and someone would catch the whirling earth? When did you begin to watch yourself, rate your performance, take yourself with deadly seriousness? When did you begin to plot your strategy to avoid the laughter and the whispers of others? When did you become the king or the queen? It's a wearisome business, isn't it?

"Control yourself!" Of course, there are times for that, but finally there is something faithless in it. If we leap, will the earth disappear and leave us stranded? Will we do a prat fall and wish the earth would swallow us? What are we afraid will happen if we lose control of ourselves? It is a terrible thing to have to watch yourself all the time. Yet that is what it means to be the king or queen, if you take it too seriously, if you believe the worst that others might believe about you. Then you have to control that worst. You have to control whatever could be seen by dagger eyes as foolish, or crude, or bold, or just different. Don't take chances that could lead to failure or humiliation, or to creativity and exaltation, either. Do nothing to excess—even if it is loving or trusting or enjoying or giving yourself. Never get carried away. Never be a naked truth.

I believed it all. Even while I protested, even while I argued, even while I talked about God, and love and liberty and forgiveness, some part of me believed all that about control. My feet became still, and feet tell you what a person really believes. Watch not just where but how a person's feet move, and you'll see that person's creed. Mine didn't move from the beaten path—what an apt phrase, the beaten path. I controlled myself. I put on the robe of pride, which is the crust of fear, and with that robe, became the king.

But I never danced again, with anyone. Not with Michal my wife. Not with my children. Dancing is like loving: you can't watch yourself loving or you won't be there with the one you love. You'll be detached, careful. You won't be present. You can't love unless you are naked truth to naked truth.

That day, pride began to come between me and others. I used to watch Michal's eyes, her movements. There was a hardness and a dullness in them. I wonder now if she really wanted me to believe her when she insisted *she* believed the worst about me. I wonder. She seemed trapped behind that hardness, and yet there was a certain longing in her, a wistfulness. I wonder if she didn't really want me to dance with her. But instead, I caught her fear, and when we were together, the pride of one of us clanked against the pride of the other, and the sound was hollow like the armor of two contesting warriors: the king and the queen.

The insidious thing about control is that it quickly amplifies: to controlling yourself, you add controlling others. That is characteristic of the king. Or the queen. *Any* king and queen. Control becomes defensive, actively defensive. You watch others as well as yourself. Control transposes into envy, then hostility, then overweening aggression. You need to control what goes on around you. What and who. Openly or secretly. By power or intrigue. By domination or deals. By oppression or seduction. The need to control is voracious because, inside, the fear keeps gnawing.

And that is how Bathsheba happened for me. It was less an affair of lust than of pride, though the two may be linked in some essential way. I wanted to control, to possess that beautiful woman. With charm and guile, I did possess her. Oh, it was lovely. Lovely, but addicting. I could not let her be. So I had her husband, Uriah, sent off to war, to a place in battle where I knew he'd be killed. Even the war itself was an attempt to extend my control, or that of my nation, over the enemy, the Ammonites. But that is another story. Or is it? Control feeds on itself. It is gluttonous. As is pride. We are always going off to war, are we not? Oh, yes, my efforts to control may be more obvious than yours, but surely only that— more obvious. When news of Uriah's death came, I took Bathsheba, brought her to my house, and made her my wife. But I never danced again.

Now I come to the strangest part of my story. It has to do with God. No, actually, it has to with the way we think of God. Or maybe it has to do with the way we *don't* think of God. Well, I can only tell my story. The point of it is, I want to give up control. I want to be just David.

After Bathsheba, a man named Nathan came to see me. Nathan and I had talked before. We were friends, of a sort. This time, he told me a story about a rich man who stole the only ewe lamb of a poor man. I said the rich man should be punished for doing such a thing, sentenced to death. Even as I said it, some part of me understood that I was like that rich man and believed I should be punished. Punished! Punished!

Nathan agreed. You should understand that Nathan was a strange man. He claimed to speak for God, and I do not doubt that he did, in some important way. Yet maybe not in *every* way. After all, Nathan was a man, not God. But since becoming king I had forgotten God; at least I had forgotten the God I danced with earlier. Now I was afraid, so I believed Nathan when he said that, because of what I'd done, terrible things were bound to happen to me, to my family, to my children, to the nation.

But then Nathan said a very curious thing, something that was unbelievable to me: "The Lord also has laid aside your sin."

Why was that unbelievable? I'll tell you, though you may already know. It was unbelievable because I felt unforgivable. Feeling unforgivable is simply pride inverted. What *was* believable was the punishment Nathan said God was sending to me. What *was* believable was the worst, just as it had been with Michal the day she ridiculed me for dancing before the Ark. It was *forgiveness* that was unbelievable because I had come to believe only the worst, and to consider the worst was inevitable.

So we come to think God has to do what we have to do— punish. We believe the worst about God and think we defeat Him thus. So sooner or later, the worst is bound to happen and even God cannot do anything about it. Do you understand me when I say that is pride at its most perverse?

And is not pride perverted what *really* controls us? Is not fate simply our rigidity made cosmic? Is not control something we project onto God? Therein is the strangest part of the story. The ultimate twist to our need to control is that we finally end up feeling controlled by circumstances, by fate, by God. Thereby do we not turn our need to control into God's need to control, and then feel helpless? Yes, of course!

And we all know the effect of believing something is inevitable: the effect is despair. We assume nothing new can really happen, nothing novel, nothing different. Our efforts are half-hearted and smell of defeat. I was the king, yet I watched but did not move while my wives maneuvered their sons into positions of power. I watched but did not move while my sons fought their civil wars. I watched but did not move while Absalom, my son, pursued ambition to his death, and I mourned him as I mourned myself. I watched but did not move while seeds of dissension and division were broadcast about the land. What was believable was the worst. What was unbelievable was God's forgiveness.

And you? What has become inevitable for you and for your children? What forms of war, of strife, of decay, of injustice? What? And whatever it is, do you watch and not move because what is believable is the worst? Do you understand at all the pride in that illusion—the terrible, destructive pride?

I do, because I watched and did not move. And yet, what is strangest of all is that sometimes, even then, I heard the music. Do you? I heard the music in the turning of the seasons, the song of the crickets, the wind in the sandalwood trees and the quick scent, in the scurry of leaves down the streets, in children laughing and an old man's knowing nod, in geese swimming against the moon and the sound of the shepherd's flute. I heard the music but I never danced again! Yet I kept remembering the look in Michal's eyes, the wistfulness, the look of what I think now was her wish that I had not believed her when she believed the worst about me, but instead had danced with her. But I had stopped dancing.

Yet listen to me now, listen to David, and I'll tell you a secret. God does not stop dancing. God never stops dancing. God does not believe the worst we believe about Him. Maybe that's what love is all about: not believing the worst others believe about you, or say they do. Maybe that's what it means that love forgives. So God the lover sees the wistful look in our eyes, our souls' eyes, and dances with us. ''The Lord has laid aside your sin...'' Do you believe that? Do I believe that? Or is the worst still all that is believable to us? I never danced again, but never is not over yet.

I've told my story as a clue to the secret of life: it lies in discerning what you wish you *hadn't* done before it is too late to do something different. Well, I wish I had not stopped dancing—before God, in God!

''You're a fool,'' Michal had said.

Oh, to have danced with her then, danced and said, ''Of course I'm a fool. So are you, Michal. Better to be a glad fool than to have to be the king and queen.''

Ah, we are all fools, my friends. How wonderful, how freeing to accept that. It is indeed better than having to be kings and queens. It is our foolishness that unites us—the foolishness of music, of sex, of dance, of laughter, of parties, of loving, of trusting, of believing that something new and wondrous is possible and daring to try it, be it, do it. The king controls, but a fool knows that throwing your life away is the only condition for getting it back, that self-abandon is the secret of freedom. A fool knows that to dance is to discover the earth will catch you when you leap, and Someone will catch the earth, and new things are possible—not because God controls, but because God never stops dancing. Dancing is an act of faith. Dancing is an act of forgiving.

So, please! Please, dance with me, Michal—all the Michals of the world; dance with me, Uriah—all you Uriahs I've controlled to death; all you sons and daughters, friends and enemies; all you Bathshebas and Absaloms. Dance with me, God. Oh, yes, dance with me. Yes, yes, yes!

Exuberance is risky, for it makes you vulnerable to pain. But pride is deadly, for it makes you invulnerable to love. Beloved ones, don't be afraid to disbelieve the worst. Don't be afraid to be a naked truth. Don't be afraid to believe the miracle of fools like me, like you, like God. Remember David! Remember David. . .and dance, dance, dance.

(I & II Samuel;
Matthew 1:1-18, especially verse 6)

JUST BETWEEN FRIENDS

People wonder why I did it. After they think a while about what happened, that's what they want to know. It's a good question. They are really asking about themselves, which is why it's a good question.

I didn't do it to make a name for myself, though probably no one would remember me at all if I hadn't done it. Yet, the reason I am remembered isn't so much that I did it as that the other person involved is famous. By doing what I did, I became a footnote in King David's history. More importantly, I became a footnote in God's history. But it was not to be remembered that I did it.

Nor did I do it because I wanted to be a leader. The desire to be a leader usually disqualifies the seeker because ambition stifles the qualities that distinguish leaders from office holders. What I did wasn't calculated to gain a following, though a few may have recognized some potential of their own in my act and been drawn to me for that reason. But most people thought I was a fool. They may have been right, in a way. What I did probably was foolhardy, but it wasn't impetuous. It was rooted in a past—my past, and surely some of God's.

And I knew there wouldn't be any material gain in it for me. It was much more likely that I would have to *pay* for what I did. Ideals, if that's what you want to call them, may get a tip of the hat but not a tip from the treasury in either the market place or the contrivances of government.

Nor was what I did a grab for power, though to some it may have looked that way because it was a grappling *with* power. What I did was go eyeball-to-eyeball with the king, not to grab power but to confront it. I was really more interested in authority than power. Without getting into a philosophical thicket, I simply mean that power is the means, the strength to move things and people around from outside. Authority is the capacity to move people inside, to gain their trust and help them liberate themselves from illusions. So what I did was to speak truth to power, as the saying goes. And I did it so I wouldn't lose my truth, my authority. My truth was all I had for myself, all I had to give anyone. In that, I am the same as you, which is why I tell this story.

My name is Nathan, and my story is simple in bare outline. I am known as a prophet, but the title is less critical than the truth: I am remembered because I had the guts to tell the King—King David, no less—that he acted immorally by using his power for his own gain. He seduced Bathsheba, got her pregnant, tried to manipulate her husband, Uriah, a poor soldier in his army, into taking the responsibility for the pregnancy. When he couldn't compromise Uriah, David arranged with one of his military advisors to have Uriah killed in battle. When news of Uriah's death came, David, in the blindness of his passion, ordered that Bathsheba be moved into his quarters in the palace.

So I went to David and told him he couldn't get away with what he had done to betray us and himself. I eased into it by telling him a story about a rich man stealing a poor man's only lamb. When David got righteously angry at the rich man and wanted to nail his hide to the wall, I said, "David, you are the man." Beneath his royal accouterments, I knew that David struggled with himself, with moral issues, with God. I knew his guilt would be gnawing at him. So, being smart and sensitive, I gambled that David would get the point. He did. He made no excuses, no denials, no protests at what I told him would be the consequences of his betrayal. To his credit, David was truly contrite. So, ostensibly, the story ends. At least the end of what most people recall, if they recall the story at all.

But to end my story there makes it only an interesting interlude, perhaps vaguely instructive, confined to an outmoded piece of history. In fact, by being dismissed as irrelevant, my story is relegated to the genre of entertainment. Over the years a few books have been written and one or two movies made about it, which further identifies my story as mere entertainment, nothing more, and implies that it is essentially unreal and, for times such as this, hopelessly simplistic. But I can assure you that there is nothing unreal or simplistic about going belly-up to the king—any more than there would be about going belly-up to the president, or the Chief Executive Officer, or the manager, or supervisor, or whoever holds sway in your life. You don't risk your life for a platitude.

So let me start again. My name is Nathan. I desperately want you to know me. If I am fanatic about *anything*, it is about being realistic. I think the only true realists are idealists, those who understand that another, higher reality impinges on this one. In that ultimate sense, I am profoundly realistic. And relevant. And motivated by a sense of urgency. So attend well to me!

Begin with this because it's the primary sticking point: I'm no different than other human beings—same struggles, same fears, same dreams, same needs. To dismiss me by saying I'm a prophet, as if that makes me some other kind of species than human, is to kid yourself. Unfortunately, self-deception is easy. It is a common way to side step yourself with breathtaking agility.

A not-small-part of what I wanted as a human being was to be liked. And I also wanted to stay out of trouble and live my life as well and peacefully as I could. In that we're alike, I suspect. But I ask you, is that realistic or is that fantasy? Who cares to have a cipher as a friend? Who needs a Yes man if No is what needs saying? I learned early that there is such a thing as wanting too much to be liked.

Something else you need to know is that David was my friend. We'd met together many times to talk about important things—and some perhaps not so important, though, honestly, it is nearly impossible to tell the difference. In truth, if you are too sure about the difference, that may be where the trouble starts. Is family, or music, or poetry, or good places to find berries or go fishing, really less important than financial deals and affairs of state?

I can say that, like almost everyone else, I loved David, and our friendship was at least as important to me as his being king. And I wanted David to like me. Certainly, I didn't want to make trouble for him or, equally to the point, I didn't want him to make trouble for me, which he could easily do, being king.

But that is the point, the realistic point, and it holds in every age. It was exactly because I *didn't* want to make trouble, or get into trouble, that I went to David and told him he was messing up. He needed to be confronted for his own sake. What kind of friend would I have been, what kind of compatriot would I have been if I had opted out on telling him? That would have been more trouble for him. And, of course, more trouble for me because I would have lost whatever makes me an honest-to-God human being.

What's more, David needed to be confronted for the nation's sake. Someone said a wink is as good as a nod to a blind man. But, no matter who he is, or how beloved, or powerful, if a person is acting blind, and making trouble for other people, you can't just wink and nod if you want to be realistic and relevant. You have to speak. As the adage goes, sometimes silence may be golden, but sometimes it is just yellow. The time comes when you have to break the collaborative silence. You have to act. If you don't, it's more trouble for everyone.

Which brings me to the gut issue: I had to confront David for *my* sake. When you trim the fat of soft aggrandizement and skim the froth of moralism away, either you claim your core or you squish and burp toward vacancy. But it isn't easy to make that claim. Deception is a diet to which most human beings are addicted. Confronting yourself is a form of faith, and it is hard. But that's what you have to do before you confront anyone else. I mean, *anyone* else.

I've emphasized that I wanted to be liked! I wanted David to like me. I even wanted the people who *didn't* like David to like me. I confess that I also want you—*and* people who don't like you—to like me. Isn't that why we make alliances behind other people's backs? So, you learn how to seduce people into liking you by not stepping on their toes—especially if they're your friends. You try to go along with the program. Or, if it comes to that and you can't go along with the program, you slip off and find a program you *can* go along with. You avoid conflict, accentuate the comfortable, eliminate the troublesome, maximize the pleasurable—and forfeit your identity.

You see, it occurred to me along the way of "going along," that if I wanted someone to like me, I'd better make sure it was *me* they liked—not just some illusion, not some song and dance act. And I'd better make sure it was me *I* liked.

It might all have begun with David's infidelity with Bathsheba. The tangled web always begins with deceit, with being unfaithful. But there is hot-blooded infidelity, and there is cold-blooded infidelity. Cold-blooded infidelity is the indifference which slowly leaks into no difference, which is chaos. It was cold-blooded infidelity I'd have been guilty of if I hadn't let David know what I thought of what he'd done. If I hadn't cared enough to face him, I'd have killed him in some spiritual way, just as he'd killed Uriah physically. I'd also have killed something about me; I'd have been unfaithful to myself which is the first betrayal from which all others follow.

So I went to confront my friend. Now I won't lie to you: confrontation is always difficult and frightening. David was my friend, but he also had power. So I was doubly afraid. There was the strong possibility that I'd lose David as a friend. And the odds were also high that he might ridicule me, cause me to lose my credibility. Even worse, he might throw me in prison, force me into exile or have me killed as a disloyal subject.

Now, impressions are often more powerful than information. Knowing that, we create the impressions we want others to get so they won't know what seems to us weak or contemptible about us. We create the impression that we are braver or wiser than we are. That's how the worm of pride begins to eat at the core of us.

Since I was a prophet, a label which others have given me and in which I conspired, the impression may have been created that I never hesitated, that God sent me and I *went*, simple as that. It is an impression that gives status to the prophet and an excuse to those who do not want to confront themselves, or others, with their truths.

But let me tell you, God isn't a bully and I'm not a puppet. So I hesitated. I started to knock on David's door and lowered my fist a dozen times. A dozen times I turned away and argued with myself. It was an interior battle not known by others, but I tell of it now lest the unfortunate impression continue to be perpetuated that faithfulness comes easy to certain people, and the rest can let it go.

Knowing I struggled will probably disturb you. If I don't have some special traits, some clear certitude about God, then I'm no different from you or anyone else. And if I am no different from anyone else, then *none* of us has an excuse for not bellying-up to power, not confronting the oppressors in and around us. Well, there are no excuses. There are just casualties.

So attend to me! A dozen times I raised my fist to knock on David's door. A dozen times I lowered my fist and argued with myself. So I can tell you that confronting yourself is harder than confronting someone else, harder than confronting the king, or the employer, or the parent or spouse, or racist or sexist, or the raging patriot or the compliant victim.

It finally came down to what I believed. I kept asking myself, "Nathan, who *are* you?" That is a terrifying but liberating question to ask yourself. It took me what seemed forever, my fist poised on David's door, before I came up with an answer. I kept coming up with a lot of partial answers, like "Nathan, you're a husband, a father; Nathan, you're a Jew, a religious man, a decent, law-abiding citizen; Nathan, you're a helper in the community, a good man." Only none of those answers quite did it for me.

Then, almost out of the blue, I asked myself, "Nathan, what will you take a risk for, a *real* risk?"

Right then, the way my stomach squeezed up, I knew I'd hit on something basic, a way to find out who I really was. Because what you'd take a risk for is what you live for. If something doesn't matter, then there is no risk involved in it. But if something *matters*, it involves risks. What you'd take risks for—risks to create, to live out—reflects what you believe about life. And what you believe about life, ultimately, is what you believe about God. So what you risk for really lets you know who you are.

Attend carefully now, for I have come to the heart of the matter. There is an ancient truth in the tradition of my people in which God says, "I am God and you are my witnesses; if you are not my witnesses, then I am not God." I realized *that* truth is something I would risk for. That's why I turned and raised my hand the thirteenth time and knocked on David's door: God had to be God! Because if God is not God, then who am I? I mean, really, who *am* I? A piece of bone, a bit of flesh, a hank of hair. . .dust, no more! If God is not God, then who is David? Who are you? Who are any of us? If God is not God, who *cares* who I am or who you are?

We must witness to each other, else love is not love; else God is not God—at least in any way that matters to us, however God may be God in His own interior way. We must witness to each other of God or it's everyone for themselves and the Devil take the hindmost: literally, the Devil take Bathsheba, take Uriah, take me, take you, take whoever is weak or poor or powerless; finally the Devil, or the abyss, take us all.

I know. . .no one these days actually assigns people to the Devil. We're all too polite. Nobody says, "To hell with blacks and the poor and women, to hell with the people of underdeveloped nations, to hell with you, my friend, and so to hell with me." Oh no, everyone is too polite for that. And yet we do say, "To hell with our enemies," which actually amounts to almost the same thing because it is only a small jiggle from discrete inattention to malignant hostility. In any case, the consequences are the same.

So even if you do not clearly say, "To hell with you," still, all you have to do is shut up, or slink and blink away, or persuade yourself that all you're doing is avoiding trouble, or that you don't have time. . .and you really are saying to hell with it.

"I am God and you are my witnesses; if you are not my witnesses, then I am not God." That truth haunts me. My desire, my vocation as a prophet is to get you to be haunted by it, too, haunted so insistently that you will come to see that being witness to God is also your hope, your peace, your salvation.

And what is it to witness but to tell *your* truth, be your truth to someone—to friend, yes, but to foe as well, and discovering there is little difference at last? So I knocked on my own door—or God did. And then I knocked on David's door. And I kept knocking, because I stayed with him until he died.

My name is Nathan. I've tried to tell you why I did what I did, so your question about yourself might begin to be answered. Maybe next time you'll remember that if you really want to know God, you have to risk answering the knock on the door of your own soul, and then risk living your life by knocking on other people's doors. Finally, you have to risk because God can only be God *for* the real you, *through* the real you. That's what I told David. "You are the man!" Mysteriously—or maybe not so mysteriously, after our encounter—in spite of his personal troubles and the problems of our nation, David never forgot who he was. And now I say to you, as does the One to whom I witness, "You are the man. You are the woman. You are My witness."

(II Samuel 11 and 12)

SECRETS

I am Gomer. You don't remember me, do you? I didn't expect you to, actually. Most people have heard of my husband though, but that's just the way it works, isn't it? Women are not usually so well remembered by name. By looks, maybe. Or by other. . .talents, shall we say. Which is why you might remember me. You might know me by reputation. Think hard: Gomer of Israel in the days of Jereboam the King; Gomer, the daughter of Diblaim; Gomer, the wife of Hosea; Gomer, the hooker, the harlot. Ah yes, now you dimly recognize me. Now you are curious. Now you want to know more. All right, I'll tell you, though I suppose you consider it embarrassing for a woman with my reputation to address you, to approach persons of propriety, of *religious* propriety, if that's not a redundancy.

Oh yes, I'm being improper, aren't I, and everything must be in place. Women: by day, bearers of wood and water; by night, bearers of seeds and secrets. Surely it can't be wood or water or seeds you fear; it must be the secrets. Oh yes, everything must be kept in its proper place so as not to desecrate—or should I really say embarrass—anyone or anything deemed sacred. So secrets must stay in shadows and, apparently, the bearers of secrets, too!

But is that truly where we belong? In the mazed, dark interior, under the sheen of carefully rubbed deceits? Buried, but not dead? Secrets out of sight, but not of mind; out of hearing, but not of haunting? Is that our place, we secret bearers? Well, I say, "No!" And

125

so I dare to speak! You see, my friends—surely we are friends, aren't we?—it is our secrets that we have in common. It is our secrets that *make* us common, not so much in the sense of being cheap or vulgar as in the sense of being plentiful, of sharing the common human condition. Your secrets are no different from mine except in ways that do not matter, the boring details of which we grow too proud. It is not the secrets but the fear of them that buries us!

Still, you may protest that you have little in common with me and refer to my reputation to support your disclaimer. Yet it is precisely my reputation, and how I came by it, that interests you, isn't it? Of course, it is! That's one of your secrets, isn't it! So pay attention, and I will tell you something about us.

Yes, I am a whore. I know, it's an ugly word, "whore." No one will argue that. But that's not the end of it, only the beginning. Why did I become a whore? Why did I turn to harlotry, if that is what it really was? There's the question. Does anyone truly know why he is or what she is? Do you? Is it heredity? Environment? Circumstance? Chance? Or choice? To some degree it is all of these, but choice is the critical factor, and we cannot escape or excuse ourselves from that. We choose for reasons which, however vague, somehow at that moment seem compelling to us. Then, for different reasons, others will condemn us for our choices about which we then become defensive. It's a cruel game we play, being quick and eloquent in judging one another while becoming mind-tied and stutter-hearted when it comes to self-knowledge, to honestly confronting the "why" of our own self.

Perhaps evil is really only good damned up, withheld; a gift turned inside out; a wrong turn taken. But who actually does the damning, the turning, the taking? Mommy? Daddy? Siblings? Mate? Of course, all have a part, a significant part. Yet if we are determined by others, there is no chance for us, no freedom to be different. And freedom, with all its burdens and benefits, is also the human condition we are not so easily shuck of. So finally, who but you makes the choice...and so are what you choose? For if the secrets we bear are not our own—our doing, thinking, feeling own— why would we fear them so and try to bury them in some dark, psychic catacomb away from awareness and knowledge? But we *do* know, don't we, for your secrets are no different from mine, nor you from me.

Why did I become a harlot, a hooker, a whore? It was a choice, but not a choice once made, a single yes or no. It was a choice made in bits and pieces. That's the seduction of little choices, small corruptions. Each time they seem so insignificant, you don't see how they matter, until one day, all put together, you find the larger choice already made, cast from the fragments of a thousand prior nods and shrugs, each choice having eliminated its options. I was a whore by choices, you might say!

I wanted something. That's how it started, with something wanted, something calling, a restless thing, a kind of dream. A dream of gay laughter and tinkling sounds, of rustling silks and lute music and sweet, sweet smells. . .and lovers, lovers all loving me; a dream of having great knowledge and being witty-wise in fire-warmed rooms on crinkly cold nights and soft snow falling and red wine pouring. . .and lovers, lovers all loving me; a dream of moonlit seas and sailing ships and silver goblets and summer breezes. . .and lovers, all loving me. Such dreams! They were a seduction in themselves. Of course, they were young dreams. But dreams don't change with age; only our distance from them changes. Dreams stay young and we grow old, mocked by our seducers. Your secrets are no different from mine.

And when you want something badly enough, you find reasons—oh such *good* reasons—why you just must have it, why it's only true and right to have it. You find reasons, and the reasons justify the ways, so you can keep your pride while losing your virtue. So it was that I made my way, learning what to wear and what to say, learning the dance to dance and the song to sing, learning the prayer to pray to have my dream come falsely true.

Or truly false would be a better way to say what happened, for I had many lovers, but they were all not loving me. Love became a parody, a hollow thing, and I was very lonely. I'd become a product, not a person, and lovers paid for my pains!

Why do we say men pay women for their *favors*? They pay women for their pains. I do not judge men: I accepted the pay they offered. And more, up close I saw the pay they offered was out of their own pain. For their pain I was vengefully, momentarily glad; yet, quickly, the realization that my pain was not deliciously my own as a woman made me resentful, then pevish. So dawned the hard truth of the truly false dream: we pay with pain for each other's pain. And the pay is never spent, for the pain remains when we learn that the love we sought cannot be bought.

But then why do we wonder or complain if, by selling our self to gain some advantage, we lose our self? That's the deal I made, and I got paid for my pains. Hookers always do: in jewels and coin, and in the illusions of warmth, of love. My dream came truly false. And the hard truth of the truly false dream is that we are all hookers in some way. And we all get paid one way or another, paid for selling our self with a lie, a silence, a compromise to gain some advantage: promotion, raise, security, status, a few moments with another body, another person, maybe a conversation. We're seducers seduced by our own seduction; paid for our pains, though the pain remains. Your secrets are no different from mine!

So we're lost and lonely, ensnarled in the webs we weave with so many sweet nothings and silky deceits! How do we escape? Run! I did! Running, always running; running away from what I couldn't—wouldn't—face, the awful disappointment of being what I was. Running, always running...after what? I didn't know for sure. What drove me was the hope that maybe the next time, at the next corner, in the next deal, with the next lover, I would find whatever I was looking for and, if I did, would recognize it.

So I ran, tugging sleeves and tapping shoulders. ''Please! Please, stay with me, if not for pleasure, then for company.'' For, most of the time, the desire, the search was just to have someone next to me, someone turning, breathing in the night; a hand to hold, a voice to hear. It helped, for a time, to dull the pain. That's the secret. We seek each other in a thousand seductive ways, play the game with a thousand clever ploys, not so much for pleasure as just for company. Harlotry is the price we pay for making ourselves company, for company. Company is a shallow thing. A nice, shallow thing. A proper, nice, shallow thing.

But underneath is the memory of what might have been, what still might be, if the hard truth could burn off the fog of the truly false dream. What we want is life, not death. What we want is something honest: a sharing of our wounds and wonder, an opening of our spirit, a sanctuary for our secrets, an intercourse of the heart, the conception of life. Your secrets are no different from mine.

Yet I, a whore, was also the wife of Hosea, the prophet. Yes, don't forget that, however much it complicates the erotic fantasy of me. I was a wife! And it was strange how it came about. One day he came to me, this man with eyes angry and deep-set, nose lifted disdainfully, shoulders confidently squared, jaw set in just the right angle of indignation. He came to me! He must have known me, as I knew him—by reputation. He was a reformer, a preacher, a spokesman for God, some said. He had the style for it, I will say that, but he was a bit too dramatic to be wholly believable. Reputations: We play up to them, don't we? Reputations: That's often the only way we know each other, isn't it? Too bad.

Of course, Hosea knew my reputation, for my name was now a household word, used by frightened parents to frighten their children. Still, I was a celebrity. I was known, and there was glamour of sorts in that. I was attractive, alluring. People recognized me, talked about me. I had a certain status, achieved in one of the only ways a woman could. At least I was not anonymous! Two reputations: Hosea's, for all that was good and holy; mine, for all that was wild and exciting. But the biggest difference was that he had a man's privilege, and I had only a woman's reputation.

Now this smug man had the arrogance to insist on marrying me! Why? I didn't know him. I'd never even seen him face to face before. Why he and me? Then I was told—not asked, *told*—with all the others gathered round to hear Hosea's searing words: "When the Lord first spoke to Hosea, the Lord said to Hosea, 'Go, take to yourself a wife of harlotry and have children of harlotry, for the land commits great harlotry by forsaking the Lord.'"* Contempt dripped like acid from the word "harlotry." The word echoed through the streets—"harlotry, harlotry, harlotry."

"Damn you and your hurtful, arrogant words," I thought. "I am a human being, not just some public spectacle! You've come

---

*Hosea 1:2, RSV

here not to ask me to be your wife, but to make me some grand example because of my reputation. You just see in me what all of us, including you, have labored long to hide: the desires and deeds consigned to solitary dark inside; buried, buried but not dead.''

Perhaps he saw something of that hard truth in my eyes, for he repeated, a little more softly: ''The land commits great harlotry by forsaking the Lord.''

This time he emphasized the words, ''the land.'' Hosea knew about harlotry, but he didn't know the harlot. Strangely, I found myself wishing he did. For in the ashes after the fire storm of his words, a ''me'' I'd forgotten—and forsaken—started to stir.

Forsaken. How many are the ways to betray and steal from yourself? How many ways to covet and lie, to keep just the letter of the law and not the spirit, to live your own life and let others die? How many ways to ignore the poor, the sick, the oppressed? But why worry? That's *their* lookout; you look out for yourself! That's the lesson for which there are really examples everywhere. What's whoredom, but the obvious forsaking?

Ah, butcher, baker, candlestick maker, spinners of words and deals, shakers of sabres and manipulators of people, keepers of the land whom the land keeps, polluters of rivers and air and streets, what have you forgotten about yourself? Can it be that you are just as corrupt as I? Isn't the truth, the hard truth, that your secrets are no different from mine?

Oh yes, we all find reasons and ways to get what we want, and persuade ourselves that the reasons justify the ways, so we can keep our pride while losing our virtue. Who wants to admit they're wrong? Not I! Even while protesting, I heard Hosea's words, ''The land commits great harlotry by forsaking the Lord.'' But I resisted becoming an object lesson to demonstrate another's supposed virtue. I was not interested in focusing another's vision. Still, he had privilege and I had only a reputation. I became a public example.

I, Gomer, the harlot, became wife of Hosea, the prophet. . . but more by his choosing than by mine. Hosea said he was committed to me, as God was committed to the harlot land. But to me, it was a formal thing, a demonstration not a consummation. It was not an intercourse of the heart, a mutual commitment, a mutual union. I could not—did not—accept his choosing. Why? Supposedly, it is a good feeling to be chosen, to be wanted. But what was I chosen *for*? *Why* was I chosen: To prove this man's heroic stature? To be an accessory to his virtue, the grateful—oh so grateful—beneficiary of his generous gestures, his applaudable talent, his strutting faith? Yes, that is what I thought, what I felt. The relationship did not conceive life. Children, yes, for Hosea insisted that was his duty, and mine. It was a duty he seemed to enjoy.

But when our children came, Hosea gave each a name which illustrated some lesson he insisted God wanted the people to learn. Those lessons may well have needed to be learned. But these were children, only children! Our children, my children. They were not a duty!

I screamed at him, "What happened to the joy I saw in you in the act of conception?"

He shrugged, "It was not joy. It was duty. It was the will of God."

"God does not make examples of children," I protested. "What right do you have to sacrifice our children on the altar of your crusade?"

His reply was always the same: "The people must learn."

And always I shouted, "Are you so sure this is the way?"

He turned away, and I raged and wept. Forget the dreams of lute music and rustling silks and gay laughter. There was nothing of care, of sensitivity, of love in this abuse of children, and of me. I felt demeaned by his superior attitude. I resented it and I began to roam.

Wisdom has it that women are emotional and unstable. That's not wisdom, it is gossip—male gossip. There are as many men who are emotional and unstable as there are women. Moreover, if some women are flighty, some men are phlegmatic. Boring! Stability shouldn't be confused with self-absorption, even moral or spiritual self-absorption. Nor is commitment the same as inflexibility. I felt that Hosea never saw me. So I went looking.

Still, all the while, I was curiously attracted to him. I'll admit there was a certain stubborn perversity in my resistance. I wanted what I think we all want: to be loved without strings. And yet I did not love that way myself. I even made alliances with the children against Hosea, using them in a way similar to his. So I admit, in whatever little ways I did love, I loved with strings. I loved in order to ensnare, to use, to be secure. I resented in Hosea what I had contempt for in myself, and that's the paradox of it. I could not extend to Hosea the mercy he at least spoke of offering to me.

But was it mercy or just condescension he offered? And what is condescension but an insidious variation of judgment? I wanted a sanctuary for secrets, a sharing of struggle. But Hosea was aloof and condescending. What he offered felt like judgment. So I reciprocated.

Yet I was confused. I was angry at his arrogance, at his intensity and his disguised desire for me. We shared a deep desire for each other, but it was all askew. I would not accept his choosing and rigidity anymore than he would accept my needs and criticisms. So I wandered.

The sum of it was this: I did not choose my chooser. I chose to be an adulteress. I panted after other lovers. It was like an addiction I couldn't break, an anger, a rebellion I couldn't put down...until at last it put me down. This way I ran, and that, more pleading than inviting. My desperation shaded into a sense of extreme vulnerability which darkened into an unshakable mood of anxious mortality: "Please, look at me, listen to me, stay with me. I'll do anything, if you'll just take me seriously." Steadily, my pride turned whiny. "Please...seriously...anything."

Some took the offer. They looked, all right, but not at *me*. They took me, but not seriously. The result of adultery was less guilt than despair. At last, there was only pain. And tears. Tears and lonely twilight walks in the rain where in little puddles I could see the fury that I'd come to be. There were no lovers. Everyone had become an enemy, myself foremost among them. It had come to that—I disgusted myself. Or maybe that's where it all began. Maybe all the while I was acting out my self-disgust, hoping in some curious way that through lovers loving me I could come to love myself. But it didn't happen! Does it ever?

At last, someone registered an official complaint—but only after taking my offer to spend the night. It wasn't his conscience but fear of exposure that prompted his complaint. So the authorities came. They took me to the public auction, charged me with vagrancy, with being a public nuisance to be sold to the highest bidder. I was the fulfillment of Hosea's prophecy, his ultimate example.

Day by day I stood in shame, but defiantly. I kept my shame secret, just as did those who gathered to gawk and ridicule me. I knew I had betrayed myself, but I would not let anyone make me a scapegoat for that crowd of self-righteous hypocrites. It was a public auction, but no takers ever came. They only jeered my name: "Gomer, you're a harlot, Gomer, you're a whore. You deserve to be whipped, to be stoned to death."

And I spit at them and yelled back: "Who are you talking about? Yourselves?" Then I'd point to several of them and call out their names: "Hey, Beno, Shoham, Eleazar, did you ever tell anyone about the night we spent together? Ever tell anyone how you like to pretend to be a king and order your subjects to do wicked things?" Then, just before the jailer clubbed me senseless, I would hear them accusing me of lying, calling for my death.

I wasn't lying. They had spent a night with me. Yet the point is not whether they, or you, literally had spent a night with me. The deeper point is that your secrets are no different from mine! For there are many kinds of infidelities; betrayals came in many sizes and shapes. And yet perhaps it's untrue to call infidelities, "acts of faithlessness." It is truer to say that they are really acts of faithfulness, but to the wrong things, like panting after the wrong lovers. And pant we do, after many lovers; faithful we are, to many gods.

Yes, gods! For whatever we are faithful to becomes god for us. And so, you see, everyone has as many lovers as I, as many gods. Our gallery of gods is crowded: country, race, career, class, security, family, religion, self. And we do play to them: "Please, please stay with me; I'll do anything for you." Which are your lovers, your gods? Come, now. I've told you my secrets, don't deny yours.

To whom do you play the harlot? What lovers do you pant after? To which are you faithful?

But the irony is that as our gods multiply, they also divide. They divide self from self, women from men, parent from child, young from old, race from race, rich from poor, nation from nation. Multiply and divide, divide and multiply; no lovers ever loving me, everyone an enemy, hot-blooded or cold-blooded infidelities! Is it not so? Where is justice? Where is peace? Where is community? Where is love? Do we not all know something of shame and sense deep down who is responsible for what we are ashamed of? Are we not all scared and lonely, wondering what the future will bring? Your secrets are no different from mine.

One day as I stood nearly naked on the block in the slave market, seeping rage, regret and surly defiance, the usual hum of the crowd changed pitch. It accelerated and went up an octave, from the murmur of the routine to the buzz of morbid anticipation. I recognized the sound as the signal of a crowd twitching in the awareness that it was on the verge of observing someone's humiliation, perhaps violent humiliation. Then there was the sudden vacuum of silence which was quickly filled by the smell of sweat and saliva, the curious scent of the arousal of fear and excitement. People moved away from me. The scent changed from an odor in my nostrils to a taste in my mouth. The moment stopped and would not move on, settling like a stray dog who sensed her chance, sniffed, and waited where I stood.

Slowly I turned to look, making no gesture to cover my nakedness. Hosea was pushing his way through the crowd. He was the last person I expected to see. There I was, his wife, stripped of clothes and dignity and hope, for sale cheap. Still, I felt my heart curiously lift and swell at the sight of him. I tossed my hair out of my eyes and cocked my head to the side in anticipation. Somewhere a child shrieked in a game that reared like a rock to part the stream of silence; a dog barked; a donkey brayed his obscene, mawking laughter; a man coughed, hawked, spit.

Then as I watched Hosea move ever closer through the crowd until he was only a few feet away, I began to think: "Damn him, why has he come here? To ridicule me more? To humiliate me again?

To trumpet an 'I told you so'? To unsheath another of his gleaming moral points to skewer me, and everyone else but himself?'' The old, familiar anger and resentment surged through me.

Just as I drew myself up to scream defiance at him, Hosea stopped and spoke quietly to the jailer. Hosea's face looked lined, his hair streaked with unfamiliar gray. Indeed, almost everything about him seemed different. In a flash I realized what he was doing. He was going to purchase me, take me away from this place. My first impulse was to be glad. I would be free. My second impulse was to wonder why he was doing it. Was it to make himself look good? Was it to spare himself humiliation by association? Was it more of his damn condescension? Would it really matter much if I was simply transferred from public bondage to private bondage?

I had stubbornly fought against such bondage, but in the fighting seemed only to have ensnared myself all the more. Was there no alternative for me? I whirled, turning my back to Hosea, clenching my fists, squeezing my eyes to hold back the tears.

Then Hosea stood beside me and touched my face, gently trying to lift my head to look at him. I twisted away. He waited. Finally, I looked. He *had* changed. The tracing of suffering was on his face; a compassion appeared in his eyes that had not been there before. He had softened, deepened somehow. He held my gaze and said quietly to me, only to me: ''And the Lord said to me, 'Go again, love a woman who is. . .an adulteress; even as the Lord loves the people of Israel, though they turn to other gods. . .' ''* It was a different word than I'd heard before, a different tone.

He kept searching my face. I don't know what he saw because there was a tumble of feeling in me: surprise, curiosity, tenderness, wariness. I said nothing. More quietly still he asked, ''Will you go with me?''

Even then, I said nothing. He must have taken my silence for agreement, which I think it was. He nodded, stepped down and paid the jailer for me—fifteen shekels of silver and a measure of barley. I was bemused, wondering how you measure what a person is worth. The price felt at once too much, and far too little.

---

*Hosea 3:1, RSV

"Go again, love a woman who is an adulteress." The words suggested a deeper thing than simply taking a harlot wife. There was an admission in them, a vulnerability. I felt that Hosea was with me because he wanted to be. Both of us had tears in our eyes.

Hosea climbed up on the block beside me again. The jailer unlocked my leg irons. Someone in the crowd yelled, "You're a fool, Hosea." Others joined in, shouting their agreement. As if in answer, Hosea removed his outer robe and stood with me in only his waistcloth. The jeering turned obscene. Hosea offered me his robe. His voice was husky as he asked me, "Would you like to wear this?"

I will never forget the image of him holding out his robe to me. For a long time I looked at him as he held it out. I understood a little of what it cost him to do what he was doing. My adultery had wounded his pride, but wounded pride tends to become tyrannical. But to stand with me now meant he was letting his pride die. Maybe, at last, here truly was a lover loving me, choosing me.

And yet I wondered if he knew what this was costing me. I don't think he did, for I was just beginning to know the cost myself. I knew I would have to tell him as we moved on, if we were to move on. The clearest way I could have put it was that it was costing me a convenient dependency. I had depended on Hosea as someone to blame, someone who verified my anger, justified my rebellion. I see now that was my version of pride. It generated false expectations of myself, of him, of the world. Probably of God, though I was so enraged by the way Hosea used me and the children in the name of God, that I honestly hadn't given much thought to God.

Now, it seemed, Hosea was attempting to set me free. But in that moment I realized that freedom is not something one can give to another: I had to claim freedom for myself. Love created the climate, the opportunity, but it was up to me to choose the freedom. To be free, I had to deal with my fear, give up my compulsion to find lovers who would enable me to love myself. To claim my freedom, I had to give up my dependency. I had to be able to look Hosea in the eye as his worthy, valued equal, as a person, not a reputation. Tentatively, I reached for the robe and held it in my hands.

Hosea held the robe with me for a moment, and he said again, this time so others might hear, though the words were still between us: "Go again, love a woman who. . .is an adulteress, even as the Lord loves the people of Israel, though they turn to other gods. . ."

It was as if I hadn't quite heard the words before. They had come like the sound of a lute strummed once, high in the mountains, but now were echoing, echoing. ". . .as the Lord loves the people of Israel". . .loves the people. . .loves the people. . .loves the people. Before, I don't think Hosea understood, any more than I did, how right he was about God's faithfulness to me and to Israel. Faithfulness and love. Now I sensed perhaps we'd both learned something very profound about God and love, a liberating love for both of us, for all "the people of Israel." That's what was changed about Hosea. That was why he could love. In that moment, which found a home in me, God became very real to me, as did Hosea. For the first time, really, I took a deep breath. I felt a little giddy.

In the lightheartedness of it, I suddenly recognized Hosea's robe and his nakedness as a gift of love. I moved in front of him, looked him in the eye and smiled. Still looking him in the eye, I slipped the robe around my shoulders. We stood motionless but my heart was pounding. Finally Hosea smiled. We stepped down from the block together and began the long walk home, the long walk toward freedom.

Yes, I am Gomer, and your secrets are really no different from mine.

(Hosea 1—3)

A Turn of Anger

Adultery is hard to deal with when it's not safely abstract or deliciously titillating. When it becomes a personal experience, when it happens to you, it's very painful and very deflating.

It's as deflating as a kick in the groin. Things shrink when you find out. It feels like your skin shrinks, gets tighter and tighter until it threatens to split like a lamb on a spit. Your gut shrivels into tiny knots tied from the twin cords of a loser's shame and rage. Your shoulders scrunch into the cramp of apology and excuse. What you see and hear shrinks, smaller and smaller, including your breathing, so you suck in your breath with little gasps, as if there's not enough air. Then all the little pieces everything's shrunken into seem to burst and fly apart, further and further, becoming more and more disconnected until the world is full of empty spaces, holes. Then you're lost.

When it's close to you, adultery is hard to deal with. And adultery really is closer to all of us than we realize or admit. That's why I will tell you about the way it happened for me. I am called Hosea the prophet because I learned something about adultery that is a spiritual truth, but it was an agonizingly hard learning, as is the learning of any spiritual truth.

It all began when I picked a harlot named Gomer to be my wife. Admittedly, the choice was highly unusual. Some might consider it the act of a madman. Perhaps it was. I know I can't really explain it. It was just something I had to do because I became convinced that God wanted me to take a harlot for a wife. The impulse to do it came out of my struggle with myself, and with God. I was a young man, churning with the appetites and curiosity of youth, passionate to make my own way in the world. And yet I also wanted to be faithful to the God of Abraham and Moses, the God of justice and righteousness. I agonized for hours at a time, almost in a fever, torn between my two desires.

Then, lying on my back in a field one day, I saw a vision of great light and heard a voice, which I identified at once as the voice of God, saying, "Go, take to yourself a wife of harlotry and have children of harlotry, for the land commits great harlotry by forsaking the Lord."*

My first reaction was protest, but then I saw that such an act could become a powerful symbol which would get people's attention. Effectively interpreted, taking a harlot for a wife would be a noble gesture, an arresting and public religious enactment of the way God relates to the people of my country. The protest I'd initially raised transposed immediately into the kind of delighted chuckle that follows inspiration.

Now I see just how ingenious and complex the inspiration was. In fact, it was the solution for my torment. Quite honestly, a major portion of my struggle was with my own irresistible attraction to women, and sex. It was not a prurient interest so much as perhaps an excessive one, though it did not seem excessive to me as a young man. At every chance I would watch women move, utterly fascinated with the way they swayed, stooped, pivoted, stood with arched back, breasts proudly alert, a knee bent to provocatively lift one hip; then the bemused tilt of their heads as they resumed walking, as if they were as awed as I by the incredible sensuousness of the almost but not quite out of control glide and quiver of the curves and mounds and creases of their bodies. It was as if, for me, one of the secrets of life resided in that little tremor which continued for a tiny instant in certain parts of their bodies when the rest of them had come to a stop. And then there was the beauty of their hair, their lips and eyes, the lure of their smile, the sound

---

*Hosea 1:2, RSV

of their laughter. I could not get enough of watching, of imagining, of dreaming about women.

But I was as terrified as I was fascinated by my preoccupations. I felt that I was guilty of an infidelity to a stern, demanding God. If I didn't control myself, I would be in danger of the same immorality as the people of my country who thought nothing of breaking the law of Moses by fornicating, by being promiscuous and unfaithful to each other, to say nothing of being unfaithful to God. Though I was disgusted and angered by such behavior, I broke into a sweat realizing how close I was to duplicating it, in fact as well as in fantasy.

And yet, I thought, are we not created in the image of God? Does that image not apply to both men and women? Does that image not include our sexuality? Isn't it possible that in the mutual attraction of male and female, in the beauty and mystery of sex, in the experience of its ecstasies, there is a revelation, a parallel to the deepest joy of the relationship between God and human beings? If so, then why couldn't I explore my full sexual interest and still be faithful to God? So my inner argument went on, vacillating between the agony of guilt and the exhilaration of passion.

Then came the light and the voice: "Go, take to yourself a wife of harlotry and have children of harlotry, for the land commits great harlotry by forsaking the Lord." It truly was an ingenious inspiration, a solution for my torment. I could indulge my sexuality and still be exemplary in my faithfulness because, by taking a harlot as a wife, I would be a demonstration of God's relationship with Israel. I would be a living example both of God's judgment on the people and His willingness to forgive and take them back into covenant. And such an act would also give endorsement to sex, even with a lusty and experienced partner, since it was within the bonds of matrimony.

So I took Gomer as a wife. It was no small thing to do. Some people laughed, ridiculed me for the apparent absurdity of my act. But I was not put off because, inwardly, I was drawn by the beauty and the radiant sexual appeal of Gomer and, outwardly, I defended the action as a demonstration of God's intentions with Israel. In fact, I made much of it publicly, preaching that my taking a harlot as my wife was a symbol of God taking Israel back after pursuing other lovers, so to speak, and succumbing to the seduction of other gods.

Though the laughter persisted in most quarters, others listened soberly and my reputation as a prophet grew. I was a little surprised, but gratified. Most of all, I was truly glad to be speaking on God's behalf and living this metaphor of a powerful truth. For no matter the mixture of my own motives, what I was doing was a profoundly accurate parallel to the way of God with his people. "This is how it is between God and us adulterous people," I announced. "God forgives you," I told people, "return to the Lord." And I was right. That was the wonder of it: being right and having this voluptuous woman at the same time.

But I hadn't yet grasped the full power of what I was saying, and I certainly hadn't seen how the words applied to me. Gomer had become the fulfillment of all my sexual fantasies. I approached her often, and she performed her duties as a wife with sufficient ardor to satisfy my wish to be a proficient lover. I continually reassured her that I forgave her, as God forgave the people of Israel. That reassurance became part of our sexual ritual, and I assumed she not only accepted but was grateful for my generosity of spirit. I believed my forgiveness was a constant, deserved reproach to her, as well as a reminder to alter her ways. I was encouraged when, at first, Gomer seemed to be well along in her reformation, generally being subdued and cooperative, if a bit sullen on occasion.

As our children arrived, I named each in turn by the name God gave me, each name embodying a rebuke to the people of Israel. It all seemed to be working out even better than I had envisioned. My marriage and my family became a message, a model of morality, a living example of the meaning of the covenant between God and us. My public words flowed easily, poetically. My reputation grew. I felt proud of myself in those early years.

Then one afternoon, in a state of casual, routine arousal, I approached Gomer murmuring my usual phrases of appreciation for her beauty, extolling the intoxicating smoothness of her skin and the youthful tautness of her body even after the birth of our three little children, and assuring her again of my ongoing forgiveness for her earlier, profane waywardness. Suddenly she turned on me like a lioness whose cubs are threatened.

"Stop it, you molting peacock!" she screamed. "Who are you to forgive me? You strut around dispensing that sanctimonious, self-righteous blather as if you were some different species from the rest of us. It's camel crap! You know what? Underneath all that pro-phetic pretense, you're no different from all those other men who came rutting and drooling after me before. You just dress it up with your high-sounding religious gibberish and then go ahead and exploit me any way you want because supposedly you've gotten some divine sanction for it, some moral permission. What's worse, you use the children the same way. Well, I'm sick of it: sick of you and your superior attitude, sick of your arrogant expectation that I'll grovel in endless gratitude for your patronizing forgiveness. I feel manipulated, used. Who do you think you are, pawing me and forgiving me as if you had a God-given privilege to do both, and at the same time already? Well, let me tell you something: You're just one more Israelite who has committed all this harlotry you keep talking about! Damn right you are, and you better face it. So take your forgiveness and stuff it in some sheep entrails and make a burnt offering of it. And get away from me."

She stormed out of the room. I stood there stunned, feeling stripped. Much of what she said was right. I think I'd really sensed it before, but hadn't wanted to admit that something was wrong in the way we'd been living. Our relationship hadn't been what I wanted to think it was, or the way I wanted others to see it.

Oh, there'd been certain advantages in it for me, and there was undeniably some truth in our marriage being an example of the way God related to Israel. But there was another truth I'd refused to see. Our marriage was basically just a formality, lawful but shallow, without substance. It had been cordial but without deep relationship. Even the sex was somehow lacking. What I had with Gomer wasn't really what I longed for; I wanted something more. It's difficult to find words for it, but what I wanted was naked souls, not just naked bodies. I wanted us to be together, both of us, as who we were.

Was it God who stirred up such longings in me? If it was, then why wasn't it possible for the longing to be fulfilled? And if it wasn't possible, then how could the relationship between a man and a woman be similar to the relationship between God and human beings, as my vision had implied?

For days, weeks, I wandered around in a daze.

Then it was that my wife, Gomer, committed adultery. The spiral of pain and confusion accelerated. My first reaction was shame. I saw what she had done as a reflection on me, on my prowess, if you will. I imagined people—other men—would laugh at me and make snide remarks about my not being able to satisfy my wife, keep her at home. Of course, my reaction was a further extension of my original grandiosity, my inflated ego which had already kept me from seeing Gomer as a real person in her own right, not just an extension of me. Yet my grandiosity went on to keep me from seeing myself as a real person as well, not just some male image I was supposed to live up to. Sadly, my first impulse was to reduce the whole situation to a power struggle.

Then quickly layered upon my shame was fear. I was afraid that all the things people would think and say about me were true. They would laugh at me and ridicule what I'd said. I felt exposed. I truly believed other men were better lovers, with sleeker bodies, softer beds, sweeter words, more satisfying techniques. I became a voyeur of my own fantasies, each more expansive of other men's erotic capacities, and so by comparison, each more shriveling of my own sense of adequacy, attractiveness, and worth.

To compensate, I launched into a period of frantic, defensive activity. I intensified my role as a moral spokesman, denouncing Gomer, and Israel, defending higher moral values. But the effort seemed hollow to me. I'm not saying that those values aren't important. I'm saying that I tried to use my prophetic activity as an escape from hard, relational truths about me and my life. The effort didn't succeed. Increasingly, at sunset the echo of my public words merged with the lengthening shadows to mock my personal hypocrisy. Yet my growing sense of my hypocrisy only fueled my efforts to justify myself with more activity. Thus, my fear prevailed.

After fear, as if but a darker shade of the same response, came anger. I would get even with Gomer. I would expose her, shame her. Since she had done this to me, I felt free to do the same to her. I would pursue other women, take as many lovers as I pleased. The very thought made me giddy. I imagined headier wine, wilder music, exciting nights, more beautiful women until. . .until what?

The question pounced like a cat in a dark alley, spooking me. I could pursue my fantasies until *what*? Until I found the perfect woman? Perfect according to whom? How would I know? What would "perfect" look like, sound like, act like, think like? What could a perfect woman do to change me, to make me different, to make me feel whole, valuable, secure? Could *anyone* do that? However attractive, Gomer certainly hadn't made me feel secure. Could she have? What could change things? What *is* possible for us human beings?

Those were the questions I tossed with in my empty bed, trying to answer. Where was God? I had taken a harlot for a wife, as God had instructed, but she wasn't grateful, or obedient, or faithful. She had humiliated me. She had hit me with her truth, but then had run. What was I to do?

Oh, I tried some heady wine, some ready women, but to no avail. With women, I would start with bravado, but end with some shuffling excuse. I still felt shrunken, the world was still punched full of holes. And always, those questions: "What is possible? Can things change?"

In the midst of my turbulence, this time out of the darkness, came that voice and the words: "Go. . .love a woman who is. . .an adulteress; even as the Lord loves the people of Israel, though they turn to other gods and love cakes of raisins."*

Maybe the voice was only the throbbing headache from too much wine, or the squeak of an ox cart in a quiet, pre-dawn dark street, or a neighbor's baby wanting to be fed in the middle of the night, or rain on the roof. I don't know. How does God speak anyway? How, except in some way familiar enough that we might either catch—or miss—it. Or both. However it came, I heard—or

*Hosea 3:1, RSV

145

thought I heard—God's word. But I wasn't certain what to make of it, what to do about it. What would it mean to love, not just marry, a woman? Was there love in the longing I felt for Gomer, in the loneliness I felt in her absence, in my desire to change things between us? What could change things? How could I do it? And what did this new word have to do with the relationship between God and Israel? I kept getting lost in the maze of questions.

Then one night, as I stood in my bedroom window staring at nothing, I heard a whisper: "I forgive you for forgiving me." The whisper was unmistakable. I was sure Gomer had slipped back into the house, into my room. It was her voice, and those were her words. I whirled to face her, but she was gone. I ran after her, but she was nowhere to be seen. I was confused, dizzy.

Had Gomer really been there? Was it she who had whispered? What did she mean? Why did *I* need to be forgiven? For what?

I paced. I threw myself on my couch, stared at the shadows spinning on the ceiling from the moonlight. What did I need to be forgiven *for*? Was Gomer trying to trick me? Confuse me? Drive me mad? From outside came the high squeal of a bat, the scamper of tiny mice feet on cobblestones, followed by the quick rustle of the strike and the short scream of the victim, then the far-off bark of a dog, a gust of wind banging a gate.

Then in the darkness, I heard the voice again: "How can I give you up, O Ephraim!. . .I will heal their faithlessness; I will love them freely, for my anger has turned from them."*

Who had spoken *these* words? Had Gomer slipped in again and whispered them? I ran to the door. She was not there. To the window. No one. Where had the words come from? Was it the wind? The howling dog? Or was it God? What did the words mean? I felt as if the air itself was racing away from me, pulling things apart, leaving me gasping. Who was it who would love me freely? What did that mean, anyway? Whose anger had turned: Gomer's? Mine?

Yes, my anger had turned to longing. But if I'd been talking to myself, if the words had been only mine, why did I not understand them? *Who* had said, "I forgive you for forgiving me?" Who

---

*Hosea 11:8, 14:4, RSV

had I really forgiven? And why would I need to be forgiven for forgiving? It was all madness! Or was it?

I racked my brain. I felt exhausted. I dozed, fitfully, and dreamed, a terrible dream that I was a mouse, being chased by a bat with fangs and sharp claws who screeched, "I forgive you, I forgive you. Come, let me catch you, let me catch you." I was screaming something back, but the words were lost in the wind. I woke sweating and found myself repeating over and over to myself, "Go. . .love a woman, go. . .love a woman." The words kept echoing, the voice kept insisting. "Go. . .love a woman who is. . .an adulteress; even as the Lord loves the people. . ." And then, the antiphonal echo of the other words, "I will love them freely, for my anger has turned. . .my anger has turned. . ." I rose and went to the window. This time there was absolute stillness. The moon was low in the sky, glowing softly as a contented lover, spreading shadow fingers to hush the earth. It was as if someone, somewhere, was waiting for a reply. *My* reply. I stood listening, trying to drop as deeply into myself as I could, joining whoever was waiting for my reply. What would it be?

"My anger has turned," was the only response I could think of. Then, slowly, I began to turn over in my mind all the ways that anger does turn, all the ways it disguises itself: as self-righteousness, as arrogance, as demand, as manipulation, as seduction, as rigid defensiveness, as sulky withdrawal and self-pity. Even as prophetic pronouncement and moral judgment. Even as the forgiver who puts himself or herself in an elevated position to the person forgiven. Standing there in the moonlight, I realized all of those disguises of anger killed the possibility of love. All were a trap, a form of enslavement. You either loved freely, or you didn't love at all. "Go. . .love a woman who is. . .an adulteress. . ."

I hadn't forgiven Gomer, really. I had demeaned her, bullied her. I had assumed a superior position without understanding her. . .or myself. I had been angry at her without admitting it. I struggled to understand why I was angry, to face something in myself.

Then I began to see I was angry because Gomer stood against me, somehow. Even when she had said nothing, she seemed defiant, distant, insisting on her own ways of thinking, of doing things. I realized, now, that she had to do that for her own sake. And probably for mine, really. But she didn't have to be silent, aloof, covert about it until finally she had to explode, as she had that afternoon I'd tried to approach her. She didn't have to be so destructive of us, and of herself, in standing up for herself. In that she was wrong. Her anger had turned into avoidance, and I could see how that had fed my anger, my attempts to control and manipulate her. I had assumed I had a *right* to forgive her, that forgiveness was a one-way proposition.

In the terrible, expectant stillness, the lovely, silver-moon-splintered darkness, I recognized that forgiveness could never be just a one-way thing, no matter who had done the hurting or who had been hurt. Forgiveness like that is a shackles fastened on the alleged forgiven by the supposed forgiver. It is the imposition of an unpayable debt under which the rage of the indebted forever smolders. In that moment of startling recognition, I felt the night sigh almost imperceptibly. My shoulders dropped as I sighed with the night. I had made the awaited reply. For the first time in months, I felt a certain ease. I smiled. I began to see what I had to do.

I went to my couch and laid down, hands behind my head. Maybe the problem was that Gomer and I had slipped into a thoughtless, congenial familiarity, the kind of familiarity that distorts, misleads, kills. We thought we knew each other, but we didn't. I wonder if we even knew ourselves. I certainly didn't know myself.

I had assumed an easy familiarity with Gomer. I thought I knew her: she was a harlot, and a sexual object, and a reclamation project. I had assumed she was predictable. I hadn't bothered to listen to her or pay much attention to her, except erotically.

I'd assumed an easy familiarity with myself as well. I thought of myself only as a moral man, a public figure, a spokesman for the good, for God. I never bothered telling Gomer about me, about my secrets, my struggles, my fears, my demons and dreams. I ignored all that myself because I'm not sure I wanted to know too much about myself. It would have meant admitting what Gomer had said was true: in an essential way I really had committed all the harlotry I kept accusing the Israelites of. To acknowledge that truth about myself and to share it with Gomer would have changed things, made us more. . .well, more equal. That would have been harder than the congeniality, the restless routine, the empty silence. So in our simmering, unspoken anger, we just took each other for granted—the prophet and the harlot.

Boredom had settled on us like dust on chair rungs. The fine grit of the routine covers your days and nights, and without realizing it, you give only what is necessary, no more; only what is necessary to keep the mechanisms going, the pretense up, the illusion alive while the reality dies. Sex, like many things—money, food, air and water—may be necessary. But alone on my couch in the moonlight, I understood that, without love, sex—like most things that are only necessary—becomes boring.

If you give only what is necessary, it isn't love. Nor, really, is it life. Not for the one you give it to! And not for you! Suddenly I saw that as the core of adultery. That's why adultery can happen even between people married to each other. Maybe that is what Gomer meant, or whoever was the whisperer. I did need to be forgiven for forgiving her the way I had. Maybe her anger, our anger, when it was honestly expressed, could turn things another way— toward something like freedom. Maybe the power of anger is to turn things, even itself. Maybe, for both of us, forgiveness had to do with that turning. After all, that was what the voice out of the darkness had said: "I will love them freely, for my anger has turned from them."

And then what came to me felt like a blasphemous thought: If forgiveness is never a one-way proposition, then it must not be one-way even with God. Could it be that I needed to forgive God for forgiving me, and for forgiving the people against whom I railed in my prophetic indignation, my splendid anger? Did I need to forgive God for the embarrassment, the crow-eating humiliation I felt in being forgiven for not forgiving Gomer? Did I need to turn my anger at God, for not making the world work the way I wanted it, into freedom to love? Is that what the mutual forgiveness between God and me could do: turn to love? Somehow it made sense to me. Yes, I *did* need to forgive God. Oh, I know that sounds blasphemous, but how else could I break out of the shackles of my own anger and resentment, out of my guilt and all those conventional expectations and assumptions that were involved in my own great harlotry?

I stood again at the window. It was still dark and peaceful, but the dawn was breaking. I couldn't see it, but I could hear it in the tentative singing of the birds. A cool breeze riffled the leaves ever so gently. I felt as if my fever had broken. Though slightly lightheaded, there was a curious energy and strength rising in me. I realized that to turn your anger from someone is to set them free from your control; free from your demands; free to be who they are, to give as they will. I began to grasp what it might mean for me to forgive Gomer and accept her forgiveness. And faintly I also began to grasp what it might mean for me to forgive God, to set God free to be God in some new ways for me.

The words kept coming back: "Go...love...as the Lord loves...." They seemed frightening, yet full of promise. More than anything, I wanted to give that love, and find it. But would Gomer want my love? Would she love me as well? Could it be possible that a love between us might be like God's love for us, for Israel? What if Gomer remained angry and wanted nothing to do with me? What if that voice saying, "I forgive you for forgiving me," had been only a vaporous dream of my own fever?

The prospect frightened me, but I had to find out. The voice had to be true. I had to risk the promise of it, or otherwise God would be nothing. And I would be nothing. But God just could not be nothing and neither could I. Nor could all the possibilities be nothing. My longing was too deep for that to be so, my dream too insistent, my faith too passionate. To risk the dream was my way of forgiving God, and accepting God's forgiveness. To risk the dream was to make a new exodus, to turn my anger toward freedom, and to help God heal something in the world, because it was possible I *could* learn to love. I had to try with all my heart. Seeking Gomer out was the only way I could learn what truth there was to learn from Gomer's and my adultery. "Go...love a woman..."

I'd heard where she was, in the slave market standing on the block, for sale. So I went. The market was crowded. People were gawking at the prisoners for sale—especially at Gomer, it seemed to me. She was almost naked, standing with her back to them, her head erect. Tears came to my eyes, a lump to my throat. She was beautiful. And stubbornly defiant. She was Gomer.

I started walking toward her. I knew what the crowd expected of me. I was going to disappoint them, but I hoped they would grasp, or be grasped by, what I would do. Looking at Gomer, who had turned and was looking at me, I realized that to love is to risk a very concrete act with very specific people in very particular situations. There is nothing abstract about it. It is not playing to the crowd. They would have to make their own response to what I was doing. Love is an embodiment, not a pronouncement. My love was for Gomer. What can be changed is what God changes, if we risk loving. That is the mystery I learned and have to tell you.

I went to the trader and made the deal: fifteen silver pieces and an amount of barley equal to fifteen more. When it was done, I looked up at Gomer. There was anger in her face. I mounted the steps and stood beside her. I was overcome with emotions, memories, thoughts, hopes. I'm not sure I can recall exactly what was said between us.

At first I was acutely aware of her nakedness and wanted to cover her. But it was not my place to do that. It seemed enough just to be with her. She spun away and stood with her back to me. I moved around her and gently touched her face, trying to look into her eyes. Finally, she looked at me. Her eyes were wary, smoldering, yet curious. There were also tears in them. I did then what I knew I had to, hoping she'd understand: I took off my robe and stood naked beside her, only my loincloth covering me. Wariness flickered in her eyes. I held my robe out to her. She didn't move. She just kept looking at me, waiting with what appeared to be the same sort of stillness as earlier the night had waited for my reply. I felt a strange mixture of tenderness and foolishness. I tried to find words, and what came were the words of the voice out of the darkness: "Go...love a woman...who is an adulteress..." I added in a whisper, "I, too, am an adulterer." I stumbled on, "...as the Lord loves the people..." She put her hands on my robe but didn't take it from me. But I saw a crinkle of a smile play on her lips.

I tried to ask her, "Did you...were you...last night...forgive me?" She kept waiting. I felt stupid. How could she have been in my room last night? But I had to find out. I blurted it out, in a whisper, "Did you forgive me for forgiving you?"

She said nothing, but her face softened and a smile crept lopsidedly across her mouth. Then she took the robe, and I think she nodded, ever so slightly.

"You're free," I said.

"Yes," she replied very softly. "Yes, we are." Then she slipped my robe around her.

For what seemed like a very long time, we stood facing each other. A thousand things seemed to pass wordlessly between us, each only a way of saying, "Yes. Yes! Yes, we are." Yet I was afraid to smile, fearing it might be a presumption, an offense. But her own smile held, and she did seem still to be waiting, and finally I could contain the gladness, the hope, the love no longer. I smiled.

Then she simply and definitely nodded, took my hand and turned to go with me off the block and through the crowd. It was a beginning, and this time I believed we knew a little better what we were about, and a little better what God was about.

(Hosea 1—3)

THE SIGN OF THE CALLUS

I loved my father, but I didn't understand him. I didn't understand him because I was sure he didn't understand me. The truth is, or was, that I didn't understand me either, which is why I wanted him to and couldn't understand why he didn't. Still, I loved my father in spite of it all. So I kept trying. I see now that he did, too. And underneath everything, that's what mattered.

I was fifteen then, almost sixteen, and all my life we had lived in what my father and mother felt was a strange land. But what they called their "homeland," I knew only from their descriptions, and from the customs they observed and made us children observe as well. The customs were very important to my father. I remember thinking they were more important to him than anything else, though since I'm older I see that was unfair to him. Now I realize that those customs made everything else more important than it would have been otherwise. For those customs had to do, for the most part, with religion, and with a God who seemed as remote and strange to me as the land in which we lived seemed to my father and mother.

But the so-called foreign land did not seem so foreign to me. At fifteen, almost sixteen, I had made many friends there, one in particular—a girl named Melisandree. But I knew she would not be acceptable to my father as someone I could marry one day because she was not one of us, not from our homeland. And that is what I didn't understand about my father, or think he understood about me. As a result, I felt trapped in the foreign land of myself.

But one night I began to understand a little. Though it was a long time ago, I remember it well, every detail. It is curious how that happens, how even while you are doing something almost routine, some small detail strikes you about it and somewhere inside you know that sometime in the future you will remember it and tell someone about it—your children, maybe, or grandchildren, though you are not quite sure why you will do that.

Anyway, when I turned fifteen, I began to meet my father and his friends as they returned home late from their work. I always met them at the same place, so I could walk the rest of the way with them. For the most part, we said nothing to each other, but being with them made me feel good, as if I was beginning to be a man.

That night it had grown quite dark by the time I met my father and the other two men as they arrived at the corner which marked off our section of town from the rest of the city. As always, my father nodded to me as I fell in step with him and his friends and, as always, the routine of the walk was the same: the weary silence punctuated by the scuffle of our feet on the hard, dusty ground, with an occasional terse exchange among the men. We made our way down the narrow streets flanked by small houses made of clay brick, most of them neatly kept. But they were obviously poor and shabby, and cramped with more people than they could accommodate, though there was always room for everyone, as seems to be the case in the poor section of any town.

To me, the evening air felt wondrously sensuous, perfumed by seductive cooking smells and softly rouged by the easy tone of voices which drifted from the uncovered windows. The indistinct voices were occasionally punctuated by a baby's cry, or the prickly quarrel of tired children, or the explosion of a mother whose day-long accumulation of frustration suddenly combusted. But the smells and sounds seemed exciting to me, like a young woman wearing a clinging dress with a discreet slit at just the right place to stimulate the imagination.

But if they heard the sounds or noticed the smells, my father and his friends did not acknowledge them. The men had worked until twilight on the wall near the Gate of Ishtar which guarded the entrance to Babylon on the north side of the city. While they had made their way back to their homes in the poorer section on the east side of the city, night had deepened. Even the light which came from large oil lamps in the homes of wealthier people was missing in our part of town. Yet we walked quickly, familiar with the course, dark as it had become.

The one or two candles burning in some houses gave a faint, flickering light through windows where coarse curtains had not yet been drawn against the chill of the night breeze. To me it was home, those street smells and scraps of conversation, the crying babies, the shadows, the phrases of a song you could sometimes hear some grandmother singing from memory to a memory. But it wasn't home to my father and his friends. I didn't understand. They were so tired and so absorbed in their thoughts. They didn't seem to notice anything, even the dog that barked at us and then ran off down the street.

My father, Josiah, was the largest of the three. I was surprised when he stopped for a moment, looked at the sky and broke the silence. "The stars are bright," he commented. "If the weather holds, we can finish our section of the wall in three days."

"What difference will it make?" replied the smaller and older man whose name was Amon. "Three days or thirty, it's all the same."

The third man walked with a limp and was so thin he looked sick. His name was Nathan, and he nodded in agreement with Amon. "Besides," Nathan observed, "when this section is finished, there will be another. We're caught like fish in Nebuchadnezzar's net. Why struggle? What's the hurry? Anyway, I'll leave you here. Good night, Josiah. Good night, Amon."

The men's voices were husky from their fatigue, and they ignored me altogether, which I felt to be part of the rite of accepting my company.

"Good night, Nathan," my father replied. "Yahweh's blessing on you."

Nathan only grunted in reply and gestured with his hand in a way that was a total rebuttal of all my father meant by his farewell. I smiled at Nathan's impiety. He stood a moment in the doorway of his house. "I'll be ready just before dawn," he said turning to go in, tossing the rest of his words over his shoulder. "I'll be waiting for you." He lifted the flap, stepped into the dim light of the room and was gone.

My father and Amon and I walked on in silence. After a minute, Amon said, "Nathan's right, Josiah. It's been twenty years. We're still captives in this alien land. Our work has no purpose."

"Who is to say, Amon?" my father replied. "Trust in the Lord." Often my father's religious outlook embarrassed me. I took it as passivity. Why didn't he talk of rebellion? Why didn't we try to escape?

Amon snorted. "Josiah, you live in a dream. Wake up! What's to trust? Twenty years and each day is like the next, just as each brick in Nebuchadnezzar's wall is like the next. You build the forms, we pour the clay, Nathan and his crew put them in place. Eventually wind and water and time, or some enemy's battering ram, will crumble them. And that's how it is with the years of our lives. They go nowhere, mean nothing. Face it, Josiah! If there is a God, He's long since forgotten us. My life, your life amount to no more than a dog's." Amon waved a hand at the dog who had come back to sniff warily at us.

The look on my father's face was one of great loneliness. Then he smiled and put his hand on Amon's shoulder. "My friend, you speak from weariness," he said. Gently touching Amon's head, he added, "and from here. I, too, think those thoughts at times. But, Amon, those are just thoughts, and the first duty of thinking is to recognize its own limits. We may know how to build something, but who can establish the value of what is built, or determine whether it is right to build it at all? We can plan and measure the strength of what is built, but not its beauty. Amon, thoughts are no more real than what you call my dream."

"Besides," my father continued, "as we were walking home tonight, remember how fast you jumped out of the way when that chariot went out of control and almost ran us down. Here..." my

father touched Amon's chest, ''here in your heart something tells
you life is good, that it's worth living, or you wouldn't have jumped
out of the way so quickly. Trust your heart, Amon. The Lord has
not forgotten us.''

Amon just shrugged and we started walking again. A few
steps further on, Amon spoke quietly. ''Perhaps you have a point,
Josiah. But does a fish trust the fisherman in whose net he's caught?
The heart of the fish may beat wildly, and the fish may trust the
water even while being pulled out of it. Who is the fisherman in
whose net we are caught? Is it Nebuchadnezzar? Is it Marduk, the
god of these clever Babylonians? Or is it Yahweh? All we know is
that we are the fish, and we are almost completely out of the water.
What's to trust?'' We had come to Amon's house. ''Good night,
Josiah.''

''Amon,'' my father chuckled, ''in your heart you know we
are not dogs or fish. We are human beings. We carry our water with
us, inside. Jeremiah warned us before Jerusalem fell that we would
be punished for turning away from Yahweh's law. But the punishment can refine us, make us strong. Besides, God rules over
fishermen as well as fish, Amon. Remember, there is only one God,
even if these Babylonians know Him as Marduk. Babylon will pass.
So will Nebuchadnezzar. But not God. So we must not forget
Jerusalem. We must not forget the Lord and His promises.''

Again Amon shrugged. ''Good night, Josiah,'' he said,
dismissing the subject. ''I'll be here when the morning star begins
to set.'' He stepped into his house and dropped the flap.

I was surprised that I felt disappointed. I found myself
wanting my father's words to prevail, to persuade Amon—and me
as well—and lift the gloom Amon and Nathan had spread. But my
father just hunched his shoulders against the rising wind and
walked quickly the rest of the way home. The smile he had given
his friends was gone now. In its place were sagging lines of deep
pain and fatigue. At the door to our house he paused and looked
up at the stars for a long moment, breathing deeply.

Then in a quick movement he put his arm around my
shoulder and squeezed, hard, without saying a word. How can I
explain my feeling except to say that in that moment everything

seemed all right, and I was brave and strong, and the wind smelled of hope, and the stars were on fire, and what I didn't understand didn't matter. That may have been the moment when it began to occur to me that I would remember this night and tell of it later. My father looked into my eyes for a moment, cupped my cheek in his hand, and began to smile again. Together we stepped through the sheepskin flap into the single, small room of our house.

In one corner my mother, Hannah, was stirring a pot over a small fire. On the floor my youngest sister and brother, Naomi and Caleb, were playing and laughing. Reuben and Deborah, my other brother and sister, were seated on stools drawn up to the round wooden table in the center of the room. When they saw Josiah, they all jumped and ran to greet him. "Father's home," they shouted. In the confusion little Naomi was knocked over and began to cry.

"Wait, be careful," my father said gruffly, gathering them all in one hug, while at the same time dropping to his knees beside Naomi. "Naomi's hurt." He swooped up my little sister in his arms. "There, there," he crooned, patting her on the back. "It's all right."

Naomi put her head on my father's shoulder and looked smugly at the rest of us. My father winked at us, got to his feet and began dancing around the room with Naomi. She held onto his beard with both her hands, half laughing, half squealing with fear. My father didn't always realize how big and strong he was, and how rough he became in his frolicking with us. Watching him dance so zealously with Naomi, I knew that some of his energy came out of the frustration of those earlier moments of struggle against his friends' despair. Watching my father with new understanding, I knew I would remember that night.

Finally, my father's dance took him to my mother who had been watching him with one hand on the supper pot. I think there were tears in her eyes, though maybe it was the smoke.

"Smells wonderful," my father said, sniffing the pot. "What is it?" He put Naomi down.

"Well," Hannah retorted, tossing her head. "Is it only my cooking you care for?"

"Of course," he laughed, "what else?" He smiled and looked into her eyes. Then he gathered her in his arms and kissed her.

"I managed a small piece of lamb for our supper," my mother beamed. "I spoil you."

"It's your duty," Josiah winked, reaching over to pat little Caleb who'd been following him, feeling slighted by the attention given to Naomi. When father's hand touched Caleb's cheek, he jerked and turned away, trying to keep from crying.

My father was startled. "What is it, Caleb? Did I hurt you?"

Caleb nodded shyly. Then sensing he had hurt father's feelings, he lisped an explanation: "Your hand, ith...hot," he announced solemnly.

My father looked at his hands, and slowly knelt beside Caleb. "Hot?" he asked.

"He means rough," my sister Deborah interpreted, bending over to ruffle Caleb's hair.

"Oh, of course. They *are* rough! I forget. I'm sorry, Caleb." He kissed my little brother who immediately ran off happily after Naomi.

For a moment my father studied his hands as if to decipher some secret hidden in them. The skin was thick and heavy, cracked in places. Big calluses had formed where he gripped the heavy tools used to make the wooden forms into which the liquified clay mixed with grog and straw was poured to bake into bricks for Babylon's walls.

In Jerusalem my father's family had been fairly well fixed. He delighted to tell us that we were descendants of King David and King Solomon, many generations before. Though the kingdom had divided, and the royal family had fallen on hard times, my father's branch of the family had survived and prospered. As a young man, he had been in charge of large construction crews which built big palaces and fortresses in Jerusalem. He'd been an engineer and supervisor, not a manual laborer. But when Jerusalem fell to Babylon, he and my mother, Hannah, along with thousands of other captives, had been forced to walk for long months all the way to Babylon, where he'd been conscripted to do common labor as a carpenter. His hands were the most obvious sign of the change, and his conflicting feelings played over his face as now he studied his hands. Then he looked up and saw me watching him. He also noticed that I was holding something in my hand, something I wanted to ask him about.

"What's that, Jechoniah?"

"It's just something I found in the streets today, father," I answered. "It's part of a scroll. I think it's the kind soldiers read to everyone in the market place."

My father looked interested. "How did you get it?"

"It's torn on one side," I pointed out to him. "Maybe the soldier was carrying it in his belt, and it tore loose. Anyway, I found it. Do you think it might be valuable? Look, it lists all the triumphs and virtues of Nebuchadnezzar, all his names: 'Potentate,' 'Great Sovereign,' 'King of Kings.' It says Nebuchadnezzar is the ruler of the earth and heaven."

"No," my father thundered, "you must not believe that. It is not true. Yahweh is the ruler of heaven and earth. Nebuchadnezzar is dust, the same as we are. Nothing more."

"But father," I countered, "you told Amon we are more than that. We're not dogs, not dust."

Suddenly my father looked very weary. He sat on a stool and said, hoarsely, "Jechoniah, I meant we are not *just* dust. We have God's breath in us, God's image. But we are not God. Nebuchadnezzar is not God. Yet, in a way we are dust. Yahweh alone is the life-giver, the ruler of heaven and earth."

I was not persuaded. "But Yahweh is only a word, only something you talk about. I've never seen Yahweh; it's hard to believe what you say about Him. Nebuchadnezzar is more visible, more tangible. He has armies, and palaces, and those wonderful gardens. Trumpeters go before him everywhere, and drummers, and he is carried on fine ivory litters, and has many bodyguards. He wears gold headbands and bracelets. He is powerful, father. People do what he says. He is...splendid, don't you think?"

My father jumped up, sending the stool flying. "Splendid?" he roared. "What's splendid? Nebuchadnezzar? NO! He is rich, yes. He is powerful, yes. But he is a bully, a tyrant. His armies plunder, and he keeps the poor under his heel. He is not splendid because of all his gold and palaces and perfumes and sycophants. Yahweh is splendid, and the works of Yahweh's hands are splendid.

Human beings are splendid, Jechoniah. We are splendid—your mother and I, and you and your brothers and sisters. But Nebuchadnezzar has forgotten that he is human, a creature, and not a god, and so he is not splendid. You are splendid when you know you are a work of God's hands. Do you hear me?''

As suddenly as it had arisen, the storm of him passed, and after the storm he was calm, quiet, looking at his hands which he had been pounding together and waving around. Then he whispered, almost to himself, ''These hands, they are splendid.''

I was fifteen and did not know to be quiet then. So I pressed. ''But, father, Melisandree says that even if there is such a God as Yahweh, he is God only in Israel, not in Babylon. She says Marduk is God of all Babylon and beyond. The Ishtar Gate where you are working is in honor of Marduk, isn't it?''

At that moment I became aware of how very quiet it had gotten. For all his gentleness, my father had a temper, and I realized everyone but me was holding their breath. I joined them. My father looked at me. There was a fierceness in his eyes, but I saw it was not of anger but of determination, perhaps of love. He walked across the room and picked up the stool he had knocked over, and sat down on it, his face close to mine.

''Melisandree?'' he asked, looking into my eyes quizzically. ''She is your. . .friend, isn't she? Maybe she will learn. Maybe you will learn together. Yes, I pray you will. Jechoniah, there is only one God. Only One, no matter what name people give to Him. No name captures God, and that is why we Jews have no name for God. Still, we dare to call God, Yahweh, which only means, 'I am who I am.' I work on the Gate of Ishtar, but I honor Yahweh with my work. Even a powerful king like Nebuchadnezzar cannot rule my heart. Yahweh is not just in Israel or Jerusalem, Jechoniah. He is here, too. He is in my hands. He is in my heart. . .in many hearts. . .everywhere. . .doing new things. For Yahweh also means, 'I will be what I will be.' You do not understand, but maybe one day you will learn. You and Melisandree.''

This time, I knew to be quiet because. . .well, I felt quiet.

Finally my father got up and walked to my mother. Her black hair, now streaked with gray, was pulled back from her face.

Sweat glistened on her skin. Her clear blue eyes were deepened by strange, dark questions beyond the reach of any of us. Around her eyes, time and suffering, like rain storms, were cutting little gullies, and the gathered courage of hard years was in the set of her jaw. But judging from the way my father looked at her, he saw her as more beautiful than ever. Very carefully, he rubbed the back of his hand against her cheek.

"And you, Hannah," he smiled, "what do you say about these hands?"

Tears reappeared in her eyes and glistened in the soft light. She pressed his hand against her cheek. "I love these hands," she whispered. "They are only rough on the outside. The soul that moves them is gentle. I only wish. . ." She turned away to stir the pot on the little fire.

"What?" my father urged her.

"I wish they didn't speak so of suffering," she blurted out, turning back to face him, tears trickling down her cheeks. "Why must you suffer, Josiah? Why must we all suffer like this? So many years in captivity in this strange country! We have no home. Your hands are so full of pain. I wish they weren't."

Immediately I could feel myself caught in the undertow of my mother's tears. As always, that sucked me into a whirlpool of feelings: a choking guilt, a frantic impulse to help and, finally, a smothering sense of helplessness. I knew my brothers and sisters felt the same. We watched in awkward silence as she began to spoon the stew into our wooden bowls.

My father put his hands on her shoulders, rubbing them gently as he spoke. "Hannah, your eyes, your voice, are full of pain, too. Perhaps our suffering has brought us closer than if it had been easier for us. Perhaps pain makes us aware, more gentle. Remember, as children we were taught to sing, 'A broken heart. . .O God, thou wilt not despise.'* Then, it was just a song. Perhaps it has become music now. Now we understand that something has to get broken before it gets put back together truly. Hannah, these hands must speak of hope, these calluses of love, or the labor of them is in

*Psalm 51:17, RSV

vain. Please, I need you to see that or I will go blind as well."

My mother nodded almost imperceptibly and smiled slightly, but it was enough for my father. He sighed and flexed his shoulders, trying to drain away the tension. With her eyes still fixed on my father's face, my mother said, "Time to eat, children. Bring the stools, Jechoniah. Help Naomi, Deborah. Reuben, you and Caleb take the bowls and put them on the table and don't spill."

When we were seated around the table and our hunger turned to drool in our mouths, my father made us pause for the nightly custom before meals, reciting the familiar words: " 'Hear, O Israel, the Lord is our God, one Lord; and you must love the Lord your God with all your heart and soul and strength. These commandments which I give you this day are to be kept in your heart; you shall repeat them to your children, and speak of them indoors and out-of-doors, when you lie down and when you rise.'* There," he concluded, "what Yahweh commanded is done. Even in Babylon the covenant is kept."

"By Yahweh, too?" my mother asked, as always.

"By Yahweh, too," my father replied. "We have food, don't we?"

That was the signal to eat, and almost as soon as my father and mother had put their spoons in their stew, my bowl was half empty. Reuben and Deborah were only slightly slower, and even Caleb and Naomi were absorbed in negotiating their spoons to their mouths without spilling any more stew than stubby fingers made necessary. Stuffing a piece of bread in his mouth, my father began his nightly lecture but, as usual, his words met the same fate at meals as bones and peelings. Still, he persisted in serving them. That night he said, "Children, you must understand that we are to keep Yahweh's commandments in our *hearts*. That means we do not have to be in Israel or any other place to do it. We must love God wherever we are and remember His law."

Just then Reuben pulled Deborah's hair and Deborah squealed. I looked quickly at my father, wondering if that would trigger his temper, for I knew that Deborah's squeal was the signal

---

Deuteronomy 6:4–7, NEB

that all order was lost for that night. But he was just shaking his head, wondering, I'm sure, if any of us would ever remember anything he was trying to teach us. He had good reason to wonder. Still, he smiled, though there might have been a dram of sadness in it, and looked at mother. They shrugged and settled in to observe us, conceding, I think, that the children had endured enough seriousness for one day. So the rest of the supper was typically chaotic, everyone talking and laughing and telling stories and arguing all at once. I remember it as a warm, happy time, as most of our suppers were.

After supper Deborah put Naomi to bed, Caleb got himself to bed, and Reuben and I swept up while my father helped my mother put things away. It was day's end. We were all more tired than usual, so the room became quiet quickly. All my brothers and sisters went to sleep before my father could even say the prayer before bed. He made no mention of the omission. Sometimes my father seemed strangely comfortable with his religion in the way some men seem comfortable with women, grateful for the mystery and respecting it, not pressing it too far or reducing it too much.

I had spread out my robe in my corner and laid down, watching the shadows on the ceiling, listening, not sleeping, a mixture of ease and expectation pulsing through me. My parents thought I was asleep. "Melisandree is your friend, isn't she?" my father had said, "Maybe you will learn together." His words sang in my head.

I heard my father lay their mat on the floor. I turned slightly and watched my mother do the little aimless things she always did before joining him. Finally she blew out one of the two candles in the room. I saw my father smile.

"Let the other one burn tonight," he said softly, almost as a question.

My mother returned his smile, but teasingly said, "Why? Are we so rich?"

"Tonight I am the richest man in the world," my father answered, waving his hand at all us children and ending the sweep of the room with an open-armed invitation to Hannah. "Let it burn as a sign of Yahweh's presence," he suggested.

My mother giggled and rushed quickly to lay down beside this crazy man who enveloped her in his arms. There was much whispering and giggling, and I blushed, looking away for a moment. But I kept watching, fascinated. I saw my father run his finger down my mother's nose and onto her chin.

"Your finger ith hot," she smiled at him.

"Your chin ith hot, too," he laughed. Then he kissed her on her chin and put his head on her breast. For a time they lay very quietly together, my mother stroking his hair. I thought of Melisandree.

Finally my mother asked, tentatively, "Do you really think Yahweh is here?"

"I love you," my father said quietly.

She rolled over, causing my father to raise himself on his elbow and look at her. "What does that have to do with my question?" she insisted.

"Hannah, it has everything to do with your question," my father said, pulling the lobe of her ear. "It's because I love you that I think Yahweh is here."

"I don't understand, Josiah," she said seriously, brushing his hand away.

"I don't understand either," he replied. "I just know in my bones that love and Yahweh have to be together. Where one is, the other is, or there's not much point to either. But I'm not a scholar, Hannah! I'm a carpenter," he said, pulling her to him, "and a lover."

"Wait," she protested, struggling free of his grasp. "That's another thing. You said your hands are signs of hope, not suffering. What did you mean?"

He rolled over on his back, lifted his hands up and examined them a moment in the dim light, then dropped them with a sigh. "Remember the letter Jeremiah sent to us from Jerusalem after we got here to Babylon?" he asked.

"Dimly," my mother answered. "It was so long ago."

Suddenly I felt a deep sympathy for my father. No one, not even my mother, seemed to understand the way he saw things. I knew it was hard for him.

Undaunted, he went on. "Anyway, Jeremiah said that it was really the Lord who had carried us off to Babylon because Nebuchadnezzar couldn't have done it unless Yahweh had allowed it. And Jeremiah said Yahweh wanted us to build houses here, and plant gardens, and give our children in marriage to the Babylonians. And then Jeremiah wrote that Yahweh said, 'Seek the welfare of any city to which I have carried you off and pray to the Lord for its welfare, for on its welfare your welfare will depend.'* I couldn't understand what he meant then."

"That was so long ago," my mother sighed, "and we are still here, in this awful place, cut off from our home. Jeremiah was a fool, Josiah. He had no special knowledge. Can't you see?" Pain and anger put an edge to her voice.

"I know it's been hard, Hannah," my father replied, tenderly brushing my mother's hair from her forehead, "but this is not really such an awful place. And it is our home now, even if it is not like our old home. All I have to hang onto are Jeremiah's words, so don't take them away from me. He has to be right, Hannah. There has to be a purpose in what happens to us, even if we can't understand it. Otherwise there is no sense to anything—not to the flow of the stars in heaven, or the flow of rivers on earth, or the flow of children and children's children. Maybe we're here to learn that loving means seeking the welfare of other people, even our enemies."

"But if that's so, why must we suffer to do it?" my mother argued. "I'm so tired. Why doesn't Yahweh take better care of us?"

My father didn't answer for a long time. Finally he said, "Maybe because Yahweh is not just God of us."

"What do you mean?" my mother asked in a puzzled tone.

My father sighed and said, "Well, if there's just one God, then Yahweh can't be just *our* God. He can't just take care of us. He has to take care of everyone, like we have to take care of all our children, which means sometimes everyone isn't happy, like Caleb when I danced around with Naomi. Maybe our suffering helps Yahweh take care of everything. I don't know."

---

*Jeremiah 29:7, NEB

It was quiet again for a long time. Then my father went on. "Anyway, I work hard because I hope hard. There must be a connection between Yahweh's covenant from the past and what is happening to us now and what will happen for our children in the future. There must be a connection between Yahweh's promise to be our God and our being here in Babylon, just as there's a connection between my bricks and the wall they make, and a connection between the wall and the welfare of the city. My work is somehow connected to Yahweh's work. That's my hope. I build for the future. That's what my hands show."

"But Yahweh broke the covenant," my mother insisted. "There are no more connections."

My father flared. "Hannah, *we* broke the covenant. The people did not keep Yahweh's commandments. You know that!"

"I didn't break the commandments. You didn't. Our children didn't," my mother persisted. "Why should we have to pay?"

"Because we are part of the whole people of the covenant," my father explained wearily. "It's the same as if I committed a crime. You, everyone in the family, would be affected."

"Well, anyway the covenant is broken," my mother said, lying down on her back. "Yahweh has forgotten us."

"Hannah," my father asked quietly, "did you love me more in Jerusalem than you do here in Babylon?"

After a moment my mother conceded. "No," she said, "I love you now more than ever. But life was easier then."

"Does the meaning of life depend on how easy it is?" my father asked, his question full of ache and longing.

Again my mother paused before she answered. "I don't know. Maybe the way of love is never easy."

My father turned and propped himself on his elbow, looking down at her.

"Maybe the way of hope isn't either," he said. "Maybe hope is the way of the callus." He held his hand to the light.

My mother turned to look at his hand, then looked back at his face before she spoke. "Josiah, you are such a dreamer. As far as I can see, there is no covenant. If there ever was one, it's long since broken. The rest is just your dream. Your lovely dream which amounts to no more than your calluses.''

Slowly my father lowered himself from his elbow and put his hands behind his head. Then after a few moments, he pulled out one of his hands again, looked at it closely, and began to chuckle softly. ''Maybe I am a dreamer, Hannah. I've never told you this, but sometimes when I am working, I imagine Yahweh is working, too, as hard as I am, at whatever He is building. And then I imagine Yahweh is building a new covenant of some kind, slowly, piece by piece, not just of laws but...of some kind. I don't know what it would look like. I try to imagine, but all I can think of is that it would look like love. Then I draw a blank. I can't imagine what love itself looks like. All I can think of is you, and the children, and some friends, and home, but it never quite comes clear. And then—you must never tell anyone I told you this—then I imagine that maybe...maybe Yahweh has calluses, too. Like mine. Don't laugh. Please don't laugh.''

My mother rolled over on top of him, her arms wrapped around his shoulders. Her words were a bit muffled, but I heard the first ones she whispered: ''Oh, Josiah, I'm not laughing. I'm not.'' She put her head on his chest, and he put his arms around her. They began to kiss and whisper and make certain soft, guttural sounds. The candle gave off a curious light. Slowly their breathing caught the same rhythm, and steadily it became the rhythm of their mutual movement, a movement I knew but did not know. Again the familiar mixture of fascination and embarrassment welled up in me. I didn't want to know, didn't want to look at them, and yet I wanted more than anything else to know, and could not look away. I resisted the full acceptance of my parents' engagement in an act of such passion and...commonness. Yet stronger than my resistance was my utter gladness for them and their love, and for the pleasure they shared together in this hard world. I understood, somehow, that it was a gladness for me as well. I kept thinking of Melisandree.

When stillness tip-toed back into the room, a kind of peacefulness came with it. At last my mother asked, drowsily, ''We won't go home again, will we, Josiah?''

"The ways of Yahweh are past finding out," my father whispered gently. "Anyway, home is here, here with you, with those we love."

"But we'll never make it back to Jerusalem, will we?" my mother sighed. "It's been too long for us. You don't really hope for that, do you?"

The candlelight caught my father's sad smile as he answered her. "I hope in Yahweh, but I don't know if we will go back or not. Anyway, that doesn't matter so much. Maybe our children will, or their children, in Yahweh's good time."

He remained silent for a moment, tracing her body and face with his fingers. He chuckled softly and added, "Your cheek ith hot."

She laughed playfully in return and chided him. "What do you expect?" Then she kissed him lightly and asked, "Anyway, Josiah, do you not want to go back?"

"You know I do," he answered in a faraway voice. "When I close my eyes, I still see those golden hills, and the flocks grazing on them. I still smell the vines heavy with grapes. I still see the temple in Jerusalem shining in the morning sun, still hear the sound of the shofar and the call of the priest, 'Hear, O Israel, the Lord is our God, one Lord, and you must love the Lord...'"* His voice trailed off. "But don't forget, Moses didn't get to the promised land, Hannah. He only saw it from a far-off mountain. So it's all right. Yahweh is here as surely as the light shines from that candle in the dark. Here or there, Yahweh is the Lord."

They held each other close for a long time. Then from my mother, came one last question. "Josiah, what do you think Moses saw from the mountain?"

There was such a long pause that I thought my father had fallen asleep, but then he answered in a curiously distant voice: "I don't know. What do any of us see when we look toward tomorrow, and tomorrow's tomorrow? Things we don't understand. Dreams true beyond our power to dream them. New... hopeful...things. Maybe just...little things...things...of

---

*Deuteronomy 6:4-5a, NEB

the heart. . .'' He was asleep.

Carefully, my mother moved to kiss him where his red-gray hair lay crazily on his brow. When she moved, his hand fell from her shoulder. I don't think either of them saw it, but the dancing candlelight caught the seams and whorls and cracks of his calloused hand where it fell open on the mat. Then, I don't know how, there was light spinning around the room. It must have reflected off some shining bit of mica embedded in my father's hand from the work of the day. The whirling, tiny light spun to cast a mysterious, eerie reflection on the ceiling over the heads of us ragged exiles on the east side of Babylon.

That was the night I began to understand my father a little. And even though I was only fifteen, I began to understand love, too, I think, and maybe even God. For the reflection from my father's hand seemed curiously, compellingly like a little, hopeful new star in the heavens, a dream that would someday guide us and yet-unborn generations home—home to the heart of the God beyond all names.

(Jeremiah 29:1-14;
Matthew 1:1-18, especially verse 11)

LuraMedia Publications

Marjory Zoet Bankson, BRAIDED STREAMS: Esther and a Woman's Way of Growing
(ISBN 0-931055-05-09)

SEASONS OF FRIENDSHIP: Naomi and Ruth as a Pattern *(ISBN 0-931055-41-5)*

Carolyn Stahl Bohler, PRAYER ON WINGS: A Search for Authentic Prayer
(ISBN 0-931055-72-5)

Alla Renée Bozarth, WOMANPRIEST: A Personal Odyssey *(ISBN 0-931055-51-2)*

Mary Cartledge-Hays, TO LOVE DELILAH: Claiming the Women of the Bible
(ISBN 0-931055-68-7)

Judy Dahl, RIVER OF PROMISE: Two Women's Story of Love and Adoption
(ISBN 0-931055-64-4)

Judith Duerk, CIRCLE OF STONES: Woman's Journey to Herself *(ISBN 0-931055-66-0)*

Lura Jane Geiger and Patricia Backman, BRAIDED STREAMS: Leader's Guide
(ISBN 0-931055-09-1)

Lura Jane Geiger and Susan Tobias, SEASONS OF FRIENDSHIP: Leader's Guide
(ISBN 0-931055-74-1)

Lura Jane Geiger, Sandy Landstedt, Mary Geckeler and Peggie Oury, ASTONISH ME,
YAHWEH!: A Bible Workbook-Journal *(ISBN 0-931055-01-6)*

Kenneth L. Gibble, THE GROACHER FILE: A Satirical Exposé of Detours to Faith
(ISBN 0-931055-55-5)

Ronna Fay Jevne, Ph.D. and Alexander Levitan, M.D., NO TIME FOR NONSENSE:
Self-Help for the Seriously and Chronically Ill *(ISBN 0-931055-63-6)*

Ted Loder, EAVESDROPPING ON THE ECHOES: Voices from the Old Testament
(ISBN 0-931055-42-3 HB; ISBN 0-931055-58-X PB)

GUERRILLAS OF GRACE: Prayers for the Battle *(ISBN 0-931055-04-0)*

NO ONE BUT US: Personal Reflections on Public Sanctuary *(ISBN 0-931055-08-3)*

TRACKS IN THE STRAW: Tales Spun from the Manger *(ISBN 0-931055-06-7)*

Joseph J. Luciani, Ph.D., HEALING YOUR HABITS: Introducing Directed Imagination, a
Successful Technique for Overcoming Addictive Problems *(ISBN 0-931055-71-7)*

Jacqueline McMakin with Sonya Dyer, WORKING FROM THE HEART: For Those Who
Hunger for Meaning and Satisfaction in Their Work *(ISBN 0-931055-65-2)*

Richard C. Meyer, ONE ANOTHERING: Biblical Building Blocks for Small Groups
(0-931055-73-3)

Elizabeth O'Connor, SEARCH FOR SILENCE, Revised Edition *(ISBN 0-931055-07-5)*

Donna Schaper, A BOOK OF COMMON POWER: Narratives Against the Current
(ISBN 0-931055-67-9)

SUPERWOMAN TURNS 40: The Story of One Woman's Intentions to Grow Up
(ISBN 0-931055-57-1)

Renita Weems, JUST A SISTER AWAY: A Womanist Vision of Women's Relationships in
the Bible *(ISBN 0-931055-52-0)*

*LuraMedia is a company that searches for ways to encourage personal growth, shares the excitement
of creative integrity, and believes in the power of faith to change lives.*

7060 Miramar Rd., Suite 104
San Diego, California 92121

220.9
LOD   2036

UmW Reading 1991
Christian Personhood

RELEASED

LIBRARY OF
FIRST UNITED METHODIST CHURCH
BURLINGTON, VERMONT

DEMCO